The Art of Singing

Discovering and Developing Your True Voice

The Art of Singing

Discovering and Developing Your True Voice

by Jennifer Hamady

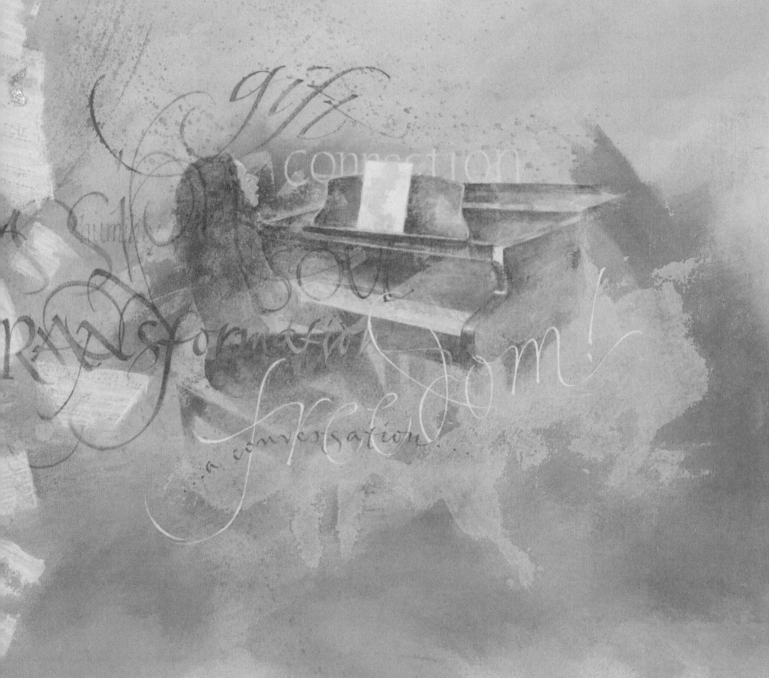

HAL•LEONARD®
CORPORATION

7777 W. BLUEMOUND RD. P.O. BOX 13819 MILWAUKEE, WI 53213

ISBN 978-1-4234-5480-9

Cover image by Randall M. Hasson

Published by:
Hal Leonard Corporation
7777 W. Bluemound Road
P.O. Box 13819
Milwaukee, WI 53213

In Australia Contact:
Hal Leonard Australia Pty. Ltd.
4 Lentara Court
Cheltenham, Victoria, 3192 Australia
Email: ausadmin@halleonard.com.au

Printed in the U.S.A.

First Edition

Visit Hal Leonard Online at
www.halleonard.com

Contents

Preface

At the end of a great conversation, we often find ourselves replaying the interaction in our minds, turning over new meanings, discovering new insights. Seeing more that could have been learned and shared together, we desire to go back and continue where we left off. We do not want the story to end.

Every time I believed this book to be done, a completed work that I felt would bring a cohesive insight, I would have a new experience—a new "aha!" discovery—that would require my returning to the moments-ago-completed draft. Sometimes it would be a simple thought, sometimes an entirely new take on a chapter I thought set in stone. The weeks and months found me adding to it like spices to a slow-cooked stew, adding little pinches and generous pours of new insights, new clients, new challenges, and all that I have been so very lucky to learn from each.

Singing is an art that is never fully mastered, never fully understood, never fully explored or experienced. Like life, it is a winding road with new surprises around each bend: something new to learn, something exciting to discover. Therefore, I offer to you what I have encountered thus far along my path. There is so much more I have to learn, so much more I hope to share… another book for another time.

Acknowledgments

This book is dedicated to my friends and family, who have always been there to support, encourage, love, and guide me in so many ways. It is dedicated to the great art of music and its transformative and healing powers on the soul and the world. It is dedicated to my clients, who have taught me more about singing, learning, life, and the power of the human spirit than I could ever have taught them. It is dedicated with gratitude to Mike Symonds for the opportunity, to Randy Hasson for the beautiful art, to Ben Culli for his guidance and excellent suggestions, and to J. Mark Baker and everyone at Hal Leonard for making this dream of mine come true.

Finally, this book is dedicated to you. Thank you for taking the time to share this conversation with me. I hope you find insights that will help you along your journey in the years to come.

Introduction

My voice has always been much more to me than just an instrument. It has been a constant companion, an unashamed communicator of my deepest feelings, a soother in times of pain and frustration, working consistently and effortlessly for as long as I can remember. To this day, a sense of wonder still overcomes me every time I sing.

Having such a great relationship with my voice, it was always difficult to relate to the vocal troubles of those around me. For years, I watched friends go to teachers desperate to learn, often to encounter hours of practice they did not seem to comprehend or necessarily benefit from. To make matters worse, each coach appeared to have a personal philosophy of how to sing properly, so finding one universally correct technique seemed to be an impossible and frustrating challenge.

I wanted to help, and became determined to find a way to communicate what felt like second nature to me. What I discovered, though, was rather startling: while I knew that my voice worked, I was not quite sure how or why. If I did not understand what I was doing to create sound effortlessly, how could I possibly explain it to anyone else?

With time, and more than a few tumultuous experiences of my own, I was able to develop an effective way to communicate the principles of beautiful and healthy singing to my friends, and eventually to my colleagues and clients. By looking not only at the voice, but also at the mind, body, and individual as a whole, a seamless and natural philosophy began to emerge, one with consistent, powerful, and long-term results.

Whether you are an award-winning vocalist or simply want to sing well in the shower, my goal is to help you discover the beauty and wonder of the voice that has always lived inside you. Beyond technical facts, we will learn together how to comprehend and utilize your instrument, and the mind that runs it, so that singing can finally become the joyful, integrated, and effortless process it was intended to be. Even if you have never sung a note in your life, the insights contained in this book about societal conditioning, learning, language, non-verbal communication, and fear will help you to establish and nurture a greater sense of self-awareness and understanding, tools that will serve you well in your every endeavor.

By looking not only at the voice, but also at the mind, body, and individual as a whole, a seamless and natural philosophy began to emerge, one with consistent, powerful, and long-term results.

The Singing World Today

Over the years, I have had many experiences that have illustrated the various and varied problematic aspects of the singing world. Here is a personal favorite:

Although Andrea Bocelli was a relative newcomer to the United States market when he made his American solo debut,[1] his passionate and emotional interpretations of the operatic repertoire had already earned him a worldwide following. At the time, I had just completed a classical university voice program, so having the opportunity to attend the concert was very exciting to me, both as a student and a fan.

The performance was spectacular. In my life, I had never seen an audience so enthralled and exuberant at a classical recital. I felt at times that I was at a football game rather than a gala performance, and I loved it! I thought, "This is true communication, this is what singing is all about: moving people to feel, celebrate, and connect to the passions inside of them."

Imagine my surprise days later when I read a horribly unflattering review in *The Washington Post*.[2] The critic went on about Bocelli's seemingly minimal training, his "thin and pallid" vocal tone, and "lazy" and "lifeless" interpretations, although I was unaware of anything in his performance to substantiate these claims. The critic's conclusion: "In short, Bocelli is a rank amateur, albeit one gifted with a few—very few—wonderful sounds." And the recital itself "proved a hype-driven and artistically dispiriting affair." He seemed completely uninterested in Bocelli's success in moving and communicating with the clearly enraptured audience, preferring to focus his praise on the accomplished, yet rigid, guest soprano to whom the audience had not responded.

I was baffled. What exactly is good singing? Is there an objective standard with which to measure it? Are experience and training more important than the performance itself? Is it possible for a singer to make people respond emotionally and, at the same time, be technically flawless?

This was not the first time I had asked these questions and felt this confusion. Singers in every genre seem to have their own perceptions and definitions of "correct" singing. Classical singers and coaches routinely claim that Broadway and pop singers using their chest voices are damaging their instruments. Pop singers, no matter how vocally consistent and powerful, seem to be incessantly criticized as flawed and unhealthy singers by Broadway and classical performers alike. And most classical singers, who often have the best understanding of breathing and vocalization techniques, frequently have a great deal of difficulty singing in any other style. To make matters worse, many singers that I have admired as vocal role models—in all genres—have periodically encountered vocal troubles requiring rest and/or surgery.

I often wondered, "Is there really only one correct style of singing, or is it possible to be musically expressive, vocally healthy, and technically correct in any and every style? If so, how?"

My Experience

After spending my youth dreaming of and preparing for a career as a professional singer, I decided, with the help of my parents' "gentle" prodding, that studying voice in college would be a good step after finishing high school. I had never had any formal vocal training, and while I was relatively certain that I was not doing anything wrong, I was eager to add to my knowledge and take my voice to new heights. I felt a technical understanding of what was already going on in my body could only help me become a better singer and musician, and I could then enter the profession of my passion armed with a complete understanding of what had always come to me so naturally.

I still remember meeting my new voice coach as if it were yesterday. She explained that I would spend the next four years learning all about support, technique, breathing, and every other skill essential to correct singing. I was thrilled. Totally in awe of this woman with a huge soprano voice, I was certain that I was on the right track.

My excitement turned to apprehension moments later when I sang for her for the first time. A few bars into my pop/Broadway rendition of "Amazing Grace,"[3] she proceeded to tell me that I should forget everything I knew about singing—that it was all wrong—and that we would be starting from scratch. The fact that my voice had worked well and predictably my whole life did not seem to interest her, nor did the fact that I could sing for hours with no fatigue, shifting easily through the registers. Still, I trusted this trained professional (She would not be there if she did not know what she was doing, right?) and looked forward to "learning how to sing." I remember thinking, "If my voice feels great now, imagine how amazing it will feel and sound when I am trained!"

Thus began an odyssey of pain and frustration as I "learned technique." Per my teacher's instructions, I gave up all non-classical singing, including studio sessions and a band that I had been in for some time. I even had to speak differently—apparently, I had been speaking incorrectly my whole life, too. Within two months of working with her, I found myself unable to sing for more than a half hour without becoming fatigued, and I was progressively losing my vocal agility. Still, the university staff encouraged me to continue. They claimed that I was using good support and technique, though I never got an explanation of either that made sense to me. I turned to my classmates for guidance, thinking maybe I was simply missing the point, but they too seemed to be lost.

After two years, my determination had turned into unabashed frustration, and my relationship with my coach was rapidly deteriorating. I started refusing to do the painful exercises she assigned me, despite her promises that my discomfort would go away with more practice. Surely I was not supposed to be in pain! Surely I was supposed to be sounding better, not worse! Surely she should be able to explain what I was doing wrong and how to fix it! No such luck. In her eyes, my lack of progress was due entirely to my inability to grasp what she had been correctly teaching.

Frightened that my future in music was evaporating but determined to finish my education and get my degree, I decided to choose a new teacher at the beginning of my junior year. There was a general sense of who the best teachers were, based on a set of criteria that included classical vocal ability, advanced degrees (in performance, not teaching), and professional operatic performance experience. These criteria put my old voice coach on the top of the list, a list that no longer interested me. What I wanted was to get my voice back. I wanted to be able to sing effortlessly and beautifully for any length of time without pain, and I was prepared to accept that I would never sing opera or have "correct technique."

I made a decision to study with a woman named Myra Tate. While she had few of the school's "top" students, her mannerisms and humble approach to each person and each voice were impressive and overwhelmingly refreshing. Among other bucked conventions, she broke the school's "classical only" cardinal rule by allowing her students to sing songs in any and every style, which was music to my pop- and Broadway-loving ears.[4]

The time I spent with Myra was transforming. Although we were not doing hours of exercises and painful scales (which I had recently come to believe was the only path to progress), we carefully worked to return my voice to its home, extricating the bad habits that had been painted on top of it to make it sound more classical and operatic. How did we do this? Simply by singing songs of my choosing in a relaxed and comfortable atmosphere. From time to time, Myra would make gentle suggestions about how to approach a certain passage or note, and then allow me to experiment on my own until I felt, understood, and internalized the information.

In time, all scales, exercises, and styles (even classical!) were comfortable and effortless. Within months, my voice was back to normal, and I was able to reconnect to the confidence and the joy of singing that had been mine before my entry into the university. I returned to my band and session work, happily got the lead in the school musical, and looked forward once again to a career in music.

People can teach only what they know.

I learned in my two years with Myra that my vocal—and personal—instincts had been accurate, and that every bit of sensory logic that I had taken as elusive and coincidental was in fact the solid foundation of technique. Training beyond this would be fine-tuning that would further open, strengthen, and expand my voice and its potential.

Myra did not necessarily have more knowledge or a better technique than my original coach. I cannot say that she was a better musician or singer, or even tell you specifically what her method was. What made Myra such an extraordinary teacher was her desire to understand how I experienced my voice, and her ability to tailor and communicate the principles of healthy singing in a way that made sense to me.

If Myra's philosophy was so effective in my case and in those of her other students, why was it (and is it still) such a challenge to find teachers who share her approach? Why do rigid, technical methods remain so popular? There are a number of reasons.

First, people can teach only what they know. Many of my university classmates (the same ones who struggled to understand their teachers' philosophies) went on to university and coaching jobs of their own. Having learned one way to sing and teach—regardless of that method's effectiveness—resulted in its conscious or unconscious repetition in some form or another, and thus the cycle continues.

Second, even if someone discovers a healthy, flawless way to sing and learn, that does not mean that they necessarily know how to communicate that philosophy to others. Some of the best singers and performers in the world freely admit that they have neither the desire nor the ability to explain the technicality of what they know perhaps only on an instinctive or intuitive level.

Sadly, many who do want to use new ideas and approaches aren't allowed the opportunity to do so. If you cannot submit a specific lesson plan and qualify your technique in an accepted way, you are less likely to get a teaching position. Myra herself was eventually replaced by a more "classical" and "qualified" coach. No matter how revolutionary or powerful their approaches and results, many coaches default to the familiar and accepted practices of the education environment in order to get a job and make a living. The result is that more teachers conform to the standard ways of teaching, regardless of their effectiveness.

With few university music schools and conservatories offering non-classical vocal degrees, young singers who desire a college education have little choice but to either enter a classical program or choose another course of study. Not only do I disagree with the standard university model of "classical and head voice only" training, I also believe it to be potentially (and often actually) harmful. Students at the traditional university age (18–21) are rarely physically ready to cultivate a true classical sound, as their voices and corresponding musculature are not fully developed. The result is generally some sort of covering, pushing, or manipulating of the natural voice production in an effort to affect a classical tone for the benefit of the material and teacher, often resulting in tensions that plague both the singer's voice and progress for years to come.

This is to say nothing of the lack of interest of many teenagers in classical repertoire, the lack of understanding of the languages in which they are sung, and the lack of opportunity to study, practice, and develop the voice and repertoire that inspired them to apply to and attend a music school in the first place. Learning new and unfamiliar material is a wonderful way to broaden a young singer's mind, but certainly not when it comes at the expense of all other styles of music.[5]

Truth #1: *Trust Your Instincts*

If you want to move a car forward, there are many ways to do it: push the car, drive the car, roll it down a hill—but certainly do not put it in reverse with the parking brake on and expect it to surge forward! Sadly, that is essentially what is happening when a student has to set aside physical, mental, and vocal frames of reference as a teacher imposes external, non-integrated techniques. Without a sense of confidence and personal empowerment, the desire to move forward cannot compete with the feeling of being hopelessly lost and stuck in reverse.

Learn to recognize, listen to, and trust your instincts, then build all knowledge and wisdom upon the rock of this foundation. As we will later discuss in detail, in essence you must become your own best teacher if you want to learn effectively. That does not mean that other people do not possess massive quantities of wisdom for you to absorb, that all university voice programs are dangerous, or that all classical singers and coaches touting technique are wrong. In fact, I have learned an immeasurable amount from classical coaches. I am simply saying that if something feels wrong, it probably is. It is imperative to trust your hunches when entering new relationships if you want them to be healthy and beneficial. This principle extends far beyond the realm of singing; always keep an open mind, honoring your instincts and yourself. You are inherently wise.

Unlearning

With my great experience with Myra under my belt, I once again felt ready to take on the musical world. What happened next was interesting.

While I never had any desire to become a coach, I continued to be drawn to my fellow singers' troubles. I ached, hearing stories of hard-earned money spent on voice lessons with little to show for it. I would get so disconcerted seeing people trying to apply "techniques" that never seemed to work consistently. In session after session, I would watch fear and anxiety ruin the performances—and the confidence—of otherwise fantastic singers.

They all want to sing freely, yet maintain control over their voices.

At the same time, people were asking how I had learned to sing in what seemed to be a comfortable and effortless way. Could I show them how to do it? My initial reaction was no, and the more I was asked, the more the walls went flying up in my face with reasons why I should not try to help other people learn to sing: "I was too young to be a teacher," "I was a singer, not a teacher," "I did not really know what I was talking about." Why would anyone pay me money to teach something that I was unable to write down and explain in a technical way? More importantly, how could I explain something that I did not even tangibly understand myself? Fortunately, people kept coming, and demand eventually overpowered my fear-related excuses.

Soon after I started coaching, I began to notice some interesting and relatively consistent patterns emerge—patterns that I still see in my clients today. They all want to sing freely, yet maintain control over their voices. They want to learn how to master the tension to create agility, understand the force that will allow flexibility, and learn to control their range of dynamic expression. These dichotomies of desire echo those I encountered in my early university years, desires completely counter-productive in learning to sing freely and beautifully.

I tried desperately to explain that tightening muscles, contorting the breath, and creating methods not integrated with natural breathing and speaking would get them nowhere. I worked hard at trying to monitor and understand exactly what my body was doing so that I could help my clients understand how to do the same. Then it occurred to me that I was trying to teach my clients what to do, when what had helped me return to my best technique was what *not* to do.

Truth #2: *Before You Learn, You Must First Unlearn*

The first step in learning to sing has nothing to do with singing or learning. You must first unlearn the bad vocal habits that you have attained throughout the course of your life.

**the end of all our exploring
will be to arrive where we started
and know the place for the first time.**[6]

—T.S. Eliot

While most people believe that learning revolves around the acquisition of new knowledge and skills, we will spend the first part of the book discussing what you may need to redefine and/or get rid of before beginning the process of true vocal development. Just as you cannot catch a beach ball if you already have one in your hands, you cannot learn new and effective techniques unless you first relax and let go of the ones that currently are not working. Most people skip this step, piling technique on top of physical tensions, rigid breathing, and pinched throats that need to be released, not educated. Only when you have removed the mental and physical bad habits that have been painted over your natural voice can you begin to develop an effective and healthy approach to your instrument.

Chapter 2

Finding the Voice
That Was Never Lost

For the great enemy of the truth is very often not the lie—deliberate, contrived, and dishonest—but the myth: persistent, persuasive, and unrealistic. Too often, we hold fast to the clichés of our forebears. We subject all facts to a prefabricated set of interpretations. We enjoy the comfort of opinion without the discomfort of thought.[1]

—John F. Kennedy

Common Misconceptions of Singing

- Singing and speaking are two completely different vocal processes.
- Most people are born with average or unattractive voices, and no amount of training could make them "great" singers.
- It takes years of training to understand and have control of your voice.
- You must practice hours upon hours to sing well.
- Understanding technique cannot come naturally; other people must teach it to you.
- Loud singing is bad for your voice.
- Singing in your chest tone (belting) is bad for your voice.
- High notes are harder to sing than low ones; you have to reach for them.
- You can sing only for a certain amount of time each day before your voice becomes hoarse and fatigued.

These and many more misconceptions of singing and the voice abound. Where do they come from and why are they so popular if they are not true? Like many accepted truths, most are tidbits of information that we have picked up casually and unconsciously from our environments and society. The problem is that unless we consciously choose to accept or reject every one that floats by, prevalent opinions turn to truths right under our noses, regardless of their veracity.

This principle extends far beyond the realm of singing. Societally conditioned belief systems abound in the arenas of work, relationships, and beauty, to name only a few. If you have not taken the time to consciously consider how you feel—and want to feel—about the world and your place in it, it is highly unlikely that you are going to stumble upon your vision. Instead, you probably will default to the systems and perceptions held by the majority of people around you.

It is difficult to create what you do not see.

Being adamant about what you do not want will not get you any closer to newer and better situations, either. Both women and men promise themselves they will not manifest certain of their parents' traits, only to observe the similarities mounting as they age. How many also swear they will never marry someone like their father or mother, yet find themselves years later saddled up next to a virtual clone of dear old dad or mom? Only by envisioning and focusing on different kinds of people and new types of relationships will you allow your mind to become truly aware of other options, each one with a description, a face, and a future.

Truth #3: *To Create, First Envision*

The same holds true for your voice. Only when you mentally establish how you want to experience singing can it become a possibility, and eventually a reality. What kind of relationship do you want to have with your voice, and with your entire body for that matter? Do you want it to be a positive and effortless one, or one fraught with conflict and insecurity? Can you envision how you would like your voice to sound and feel today? How would you like it to grow and progress over the next five years?

It is difficult to create what you do not see. With no clear idea of how you want to experience your voice and the type of relationship you want to have with it, you will almost certainly default to the prevalent notions of singing, no matter how counterproductive, frustrating, or disagreeable they may consciously seem to you. If you are certain that nothing you do will help you achieve a powerful Broadway tone or an authentic jazz sound because you have sung only country music or opera your whole life, you have sealed your fate. If you are convinced that your voice is small, you are guaranteed not to experience the freedom that comes from opening up and allowing the voice to soar with volume and strength. Your beliefs instruct the body—no matter how incorrect those beliefs might be—and no amount of practice can change a mind that has been made up.

And our minds are made up early. From the time we are in our first elementary school choir, teachers divide us into categories called soprano, alto, tenor, and bass. Even if you were put in the alto section simply because there were too many sopranos running around, you most likely began to believe that you were an alto, and therefore not a soprano.

This system of classification might be a handy way to sort singers for the benefit of performing certain choral repertoire, but it is not necessarily an accurate reflection of the physical singing apparatus. Even if you prefer to sing in a lower range, that does not mean that you cannot sing just as well and effortlessly in a higher one. Slight modifications to the way you breathe and produce sound (combined with major adjustments to the way you think) are all you need to sing notes in virtually any range. However, if you believe that you are an alto and only an alto, you will limit the number of notes you can sing, regardless of whether or not your belief is based in reality.

Realities of Singing

- Just as you can speak virtually all day every day with no fatigue or trouble, you are physically able to sing effortlessly, comfortably, and clearly with varying degrees of volume, intensity, and expression for virtually any length of time.
- Everyone has a unique tone that, when healthy and tension-free, can ring, project, and resonate in a beautiful way.
- No volume or style of singing is inherently bad for your voice.[2]
- Singing should feel as natural and comfortable as speaking, because it is as natural and comfortable as speaking.
- Many vocal problems are the result of easy-to-correct bad habits stemming from mental conditioning rather than from bad technique.
- You already possess the knowledge and ability to correct most of the problems relating to your current voice production.
- Many of your vocal problems can be resolved by redefining the language you use when dealing with your voice.
- Very few people are tone deaf.
- Going flat and singing off key are more often the result of overthinking than bad technique. When our minds and muscles are relaxed, the majority of pitch problems resolve themselves.
- You never need to reach up or down with your throat, mind, or body to hit any pitch.

"Are you sure about that?" most people respond when I run down this list, because so much of what it contains totally contradicts what we all have learned from society and our past experiences with singing.

I am sure. In day-to-day speech, the average person utilizes a range of between one and two octaves (12–24 notes). However, when asked to sing a simple scale of five notes smack dab in the middle of their speaking range, many people will tense up, tighten, and push, reinforcing the prevalent beliefs that a) singing is hard, b) only training can make it easier, and that c) the majority of people have "ugly" or "bad" voices. Many will not even attempt to sing simple songs, certain that they are either physically unable or will embarrass themselves in the process. The song "Happy Birthday" spans only an octave,[3] yet most people will strain for the "high" note, regardless of the key.

You have only one vocal mechanism: one set of lungs, one set of vocal cords, one mouth, one tongue; together, one voice. The same system you use to speak is the same and only system you have with which to sing. Logically, if you are doing one thing right (that is, speaking) with no problems, fatigue, or tensions, then singing should be no different.

When I tell my new clients this, they look at me as if I am from another planet. Most are convinced that the two processes are completely different, because of distinctions they perceive in effort required (it seems harder to sing than speak), feeling (how they have been singing feels different from how they speak), and sound.

In actuality, the main physical distinctions between speaking and singing are minor modifications that allow the singer to hold notes (sustain), amplify sound (project), and utilize nuance by affecting certain tones (color, resonance). These modifications, as well as the strengthening of the vocal mechanism, are not difficult or stressful to the body, nor are they skills that require an inherent talent with which only a few are born. Each and every one of us makes some or all of these modifications in our daily speech. We just may not be aware of it. Consider this:

- When speaking, how often do you think of breathing and the support of that breath?
- Are you aware of the movements of your diaphragm, lungs, soft palate, and arytenoids every time you utter a sound?
- Do you even know what or where your arytenoids are?[4]
- Do you pause to prepare when shifting between registers?
- Do you pause to prepare when shifting from a soft voice to a loud one?
- Are you aware of any difference in feeling between registers? Between a soft and a loud voice?
- Are you consciously hitting each of the different notes that your voice is moving between as you speak?
- Do you need to stand still and straight in order to speak comfortably, loudly, and effectively?
- Do you even need to be standing?
- Do you become hoarse after an extended conversation?

Singing well is not the implementation of foreign, complex skills.

Most likely, your answer to each of these questions is "no." You speak without a conscious thought in a variety of ways every day, just as you laugh and cry without thinking about how you create those sounds. The same way you are unaware of the vast majority of steps necessary to speak, chew, swallow, and walk, your body inherently understands what it needs to do to create tones of varying degrees of volume and power without your conscious involvement. Think of how loud and high your voice becomes when you are cheering at a concert or football game. When asked to recreate the same pitch, volume, level of intensity, and duration in the context of a song, however, many people will become nervous, tighten up, and subsequently fail.

Singing well is not the implementation of foreign, complex skills. It is learning to recognize and develop the skills that you already use unconsciously all day, every day. People whose pleasant speaking voices turn harsh and nasal during a song do not need to quit singing or spend years training to improve their tone. They mainly need to stop interfering with the very natural process of voice production that their bodies and subconscious minds mastered years ago. Simply put, they need to stop trying so hard.

If singing is truly as natural as speaking, why does it seem so difficult? Why do so many people's singing and speaking voices seem as different as night and day? Can it truly be possible that singing well is actually easy?

How We Became So Confused

Before children learn to speak, their language of communication consists of crying, laughing, sighing, cooing, and whining. Even once introduced to spoken language, most young children continue to blur the lines of sound and speech, using a sing-song style to express themselves.

Around the age of two or three, depending on the specific school and family environments, an abrupt distinction starts to form between what does and does not qualify as proper communication. Whining, crying, and even positive high-volume noises are discouraged as children are admonished to "speak like the big kids and adults." The singing and noise-making that was once encouraged and rewarded with positive attention now seem to be approved of only at certain times, the number of which continues to diminish with age. Singing in the grocery store, happy babble in the library, and coos of excitement at the movies elicit side-glances from strangers and frustrated pleas from parents to remain quiet.

Consider your own associations with a "loud" child, or how you would react to a child—yours or not—singing happily in a restaurant. I would venture a guess that most of us would feel a little annoyed or uncomfortable, rather than smile at the thought of a confident and happy kid enjoying herself. I would also venture that most of us are unaware that we are replaying the conditioning of our childhoods, now in the role of adult, because we never stopped to consciously consider that a more healthy relationship with singing and sound could exist. Do we really mind hearing singing or laughing in public, or are we simply reacting the way we have been conditioned to react?

The message that comes across to kids is, "Singing is OK. It is just not something that I should do."

I don't believe it is the sounds to which people are reacting negatively, but rather the attention that children draw in places that adults have learned to keep their voices down. Kids are not yet aware of society's rules, though, so they assume that their singing and happy noise making are the cause of the discomfort of those around them, and are therefore bad. It is in this stage that many children begin to giggle with embarrassment at singing, humming, and such, and the natural and thoughtless process of voice production is altered forever.[5]

It is interesting to note that while generation after generation of kids is taught that loud singing and expression are unacceptable in public, our society continues to admire and virtually worship those that have the courage to express themselves musically and artistically in this way. I have even seen parents hush their children for singing in the mall as they walk into the record store to buy CDs of people singing three times as loud. Think of how confusing this message must be to a child!

Whether intended or not, the message that comes across to kids is, "Singing is OK. It is just not something that I should do." As they mature, this message somehow translates to "Singing is OK. It is just not something that I have the talent to do." By the time children can understand that their parents were reacting to society's rules rather than the sound and inherent character of their specific voices, the years of conditioning have helped solidify an unfavorable relationship of their own, both mentally and physically.

Friends of mine have a daughter whose passion and talent for music (which I believe to be innate in virtually all children) was apparent before her first birthday. By the time she was two, Aida was capable of imitating speech and song with exact pitch, tone, and volume replication, frequently using her speaking and singing voices interchangeably. Even weeks after singing a song, she would return to the exact same key when singing that song again.

Her parents do not consider themselves to be musical, but their desire to nurture their daughter's joy and passion for music was stronger than their determination to keep their own mouths closed for fear of sounding bad. To this day, singing abounds in their home, and they are careful to encourage Aida's singing, at whatever volume. Consequently, Aida's relationship with her voice remains healthy and strong at the age of ten.

Some would argue that Aida has a musical gift, and that her ear and talent for music would have blossomed regardless of her upbringing. But I believe that her parents' excitement is the gift that has been the most influential in Aida's musical development thus far. While the technical aspects of language appear to be genetically influenced, the "song" and rhythm of music and language seem to be strongly affected by environment, especially prior to the ages of 7–12. Thus the importance in musical development of with whom and how you commuincate as toddler.

A number of years ago, I spent some time in Ireland and was amazed at the culture's attitude toward singing. In bars, schools, restaurants, banks, and on the street, people of all ages sang without hesitation or embarrassment. Even loud and emotional singing elicited little or no reaction from those around, and interestingly, the vast majority of these public singers sounded really great!

While this attitude is not prevalent in the United States, there are groups that regard exuberant and carefree singing as something to celebrate rather than shun. Most African-American churches I have visited have extensive music programs where singing not only does not become a self-conscious event as the members get older, but is something to take pride in. The effortlessness, power, and all-around beauty of most members' voices reflects the perception that the voice is a gift to share and celebrate. This *conditioned* outlook on the voice results in a more natural and integrated approach to singing, and thus, the tendency toward larger, more beautiful and liberated voices.

Finding Your Voice

Not all of us have or had parents like Aida's, and may find that we have unconsciously manifested unpleasant childhood experiences in our adult voices. One of my students recalled that her youthful passion for music disappeared after perpetual chastising for singing "at all the wrong times." Her single mother would come home from work stressed out and tired, and make it clear that her daughter's singing was an annoyance. Barbara was too young to understand that her mother would likely have reacted the same way to the television or radio, and therefore assumed that her voice was the problematic element.[6] To make matters worse, she was constantly told to hush by her aunt who thought loud children were disgraceful, and was singled-out by her church choir director for not blending in.

Fortunately, the effects of negative conditioning are reversible through awareness, careful and compassionate envisioning, patience, and action.

These casual and misguided comments served not only to squash Barbara's excitement about music, but to diminish her exuberant personality as well. She bought into the notion that her natural tendency to be happy, outspoken, and outgoing meant that she was unladylike, brash, and rude. These beliefs seeped into her mannerisms, confidence, and sense of self, which she carried into adulthood. No wonder she came to me with tons of throat tension and a fear of letting her singing voice—and herself—go.

It does not take negative and self-deprecating experiences to warp the way we approach our voices and singing. One of my clients grew up listening only to quiet Christian hymns because her parents felt that loud music was disrespectful to God. Luckily, she enjoyed this style of music, and eventually went on to build a career in the genre. While her voice is relatively open and comfortable, she had great difficulty willing it to produce any substantial amount of volume or emotion. Only after looking closely at the belief patterns of her upbringing was she able to consciously allow herself permission to experiment with the full scope of her vocal and emotional range.

While not everyone has quite as negative a background as Barbara's, I would venture that many of us had less-than-ideal vocal and musical experiences in our youth. Fortunately, the effects of negative conditioning are reversible through awareness, careful and compassionate envisioning, patience, and action.

The first step is to take an inventory of how you feel about singing in general, and of how you feel about your own instrument in particular. This includes the body in which your instrument is housed and the mind that controls both. Once you have done this and have established how you want your voice to feel and sound, the next step is to believe that you are powerful enough to create that relationship, regardless of how impossible it may seem based on your past experiences, current beliefs, and the opinions of other people. Then, and only then, can you develop a relationship that you have chosen consciously and proactively, rather than default to one chosen for you long ago.

Chapter 3

Language

> [Language] is not a description of reality… you can't associate each word to a thing. It's more like music. You can't say one note means anything. It's like a painting… there is no correspondence between the spots of paint and what you see in the picture. It is simply a language, referring to something that can't be stated. The reality which is most immediate to us can't be stated.[1]
>
> —David Bohm

The Way We Communicate

The purpose of language is to facilitate expression and communication, not to altogether define or contain them. As David Bohm explains, language is a vehicle to express and communicate what cannot be stated with words in its enormity and entirety. Yet, what was designed as a tool has become a crutch for many of us. The development of language and our society's reliance upon it has caused most of us to believe that all thoughts and feelings can be communicated sufficiently and effectively through speech. Nothing could be further from the truth.

The Language Two-Step

Feelings ▸ Conscious Thought ▸ Communication

Step One: Feelings ▸ Conscious Thought

Establishing a beneficial relationship with language does not begin by improving your vocabulary or diction. It begins by understanding that language is a tool to express your feelings, communicate your thoughts, and connect with others. Just as you cannot create a healthy relationship with your voice without first envisioning one, you cannot have cohesive and integrated communication habits without fully understanding what it is you feel before you decide what it is you want to say. We often skip this step, jumping in headfirst to speaking without thinking—or worse, we are not in touch with our feelings in the first place.

It is therefore not ironic that the most prevalent tool we have for expression and connection (namely, language) tends also to be a popular method of avoiding true communication. Consider the question,

"How are you?" The query and its typical response, "Fine," are uttered millions of times each day, but how often are they meant to communicate a true state of being, or inquire with genuine interest about that state? In many of our interactions, we make this type of conditioned small talk that often subverts true connection, rather than take the time and energy to engage on a more-than-cursory level.

That is not to say that you are a terrible communicator or out of touch with your feelings if you say only a casual "hello" to your neighbor or do not want to spill your guts at the water cooler. But when we develop the habit of using light chat in certain areas of our lives, it tends to migrate to other areas as well. I know people who can talk to their friends for hours without ever asking or saying how they truly feel or what they are truly thinking. I know families that insist on eating dinner together every night, though not much is being communicated when, as if from a script, the same questions and answers are repeated over and over more out of habit than sincere concern and interest.

We are so used to constant distractions that many of us find ourselves uncomfortable in the face of silence.

To make matters worse, our increasing reliance upon technology further facilitates this connection-without-communication. It has become effort-less to "stay in touch" by sending a quick email or leaving a voice message, without ever needing to communicate with someone. How many of us even prefer to get someone's voicemail, rather than actually have to talk to the person we are calling?

The prevalence of technology in our society is also responsible for keeping us relatively out of touch with ourselves. From the moment we wake up until the moment we go to sleep, the radio, the television, movies, magazines, video games, or the computer are waiting to claim our attention. We are so used to constant distractions that many of us find ourselves uncomfortable in the face of silence. But without silence, how can we hear what is really going on inside? It is virtually impossible.

Being out of touch with our thoughts and feelings means that we are less likely to be speaking about them, and the casual ties of life—schedules, deadlines, the news, bills, jobs, kids' activities, and the like—fill up our awareness. There is nothing wrong with thinking about and discussing these things, but when we focus on them primarily or exclusively, they become the foundation of our conscious experience. Thus, we enter a cycle: when we do not want to share, or are unaware of, our innermost feelings and thoughts, we speak about other things. This use of small talk in turn prevents us from taking the time to know or explore what we truly feel, and who we truly are.

Step Two : Conscious Thought ▸ Communication

Even if you are relatively in touch with your feelings and emotions and genuinely desire to connect with others on a more intimate level, you still have one more challenge to consider. Effective communication requires more than saying aloud to another person what you are thinking: effective communication requires being certain that what you say truly reflects what you feel.

This might seem like a simple step, but the majority of interpersonal breakdowns come not from unsympathetic feelings or poor intentions, but from miscommunication. In both the personal and professional realms, we frequently find ourselves reacting to something someone has said, only to later find out that they meant something entirely different.

Can it really be that hard simply to say what we think? Yes. To transfer our thoughts from the languageless realm to that of language requires more than merely that shift: it requires an act of translation. Just as translating a song or literary work from one language to another tends to slightly alter the meaning, putting our feelings into words tends to somewhat alter what we desire to communicate.

The main reason for these mistranslations is that spoken language is simply not as comprehensive as the languageless commnication of our minds and senses. Dictionaries define words like angry, beautiful, sad, happy, frustrated, joyful, peaceful, and confused in a few sentences, but the scope and nuance of their meanings are larger than what could be contained in hundreds of books. In order to communicate verbally, we fit our thoughts and feelings into these "word packages" so that we can deliver them to another person, while the greater essence remains implied rather than spoken. (This helps explain the importance of body language, eye contact, and other forms of non-verbal communication.)

In time, however, these adequate expressions of what we want to convey become sufficient for most of us, and we spend less time consciously attending to the essences, sensations, and feelings that our words are supposed to be expressing. The result is that language becomes not only our primary means of communication, but also the default method for observing and experiencing the world, a role that language was never meant to fill.

Consider the way conditioning has helped to structure your currently held language practices, and decide whether they are actually beneficial.

Consider the word "love." Perhaps one of the most glaring examples of an entire universe of meaning trapped inside a single word, there are hundreds, if not thousands, of different ways to experience love for another person. Multiply this by the number of people, animals, places, and things you care about in a lifetime and the vastness of the experience of love becomes exponential. Yet, a single word remains as our primary expression for one of the most dramatically broad emotions in human experience.

The word, love, is not the problem, just as language is not inherently the problem. The problem is when our use of a word replaces a daily reflection upon its greater, deeper, and primary meaning—that is, the sentiment and experience of love that came before the desire to express it with language. Even if we genuinely feel love for another person and want to express that love, it is very easy to fall into the habit of regurgitating the words "I love you" without really re-experiencing the emotions each time. The result is the shrinking of a powerful and constantly evolving sentiment to the stagnant size of a meager four letters.

Breaking this habit and establishing better communication habits begin with consciousness. Consider the way conditioning has helped to structure your currently held language practices, and decide whether they are actually beneficial. Assess whether what you say really reflects what you feel and think, as well as whether you are attending to your thoughts and feelings, or whether you use language consciously and unconsciously to gloss over, to downplay, or to cover up your thoughts and emotions.

Silence is a great tool, allowing us to access and experience emotions that we simply cannot with language. By dwelling in silence, the words that constantly run through our minds eventually begin to dissipate, and we are rewarded with a deeper pool of knowing. from which language can then properly emerge. I therefore encourage you to spend a few language-free days. If an entire day seems like an enormous challenge to you, begin with 15 minutes, later increasing to an hour and so forth. Though not speaking for long periods could pose a number of problems in daily living, spending time in both verbal and auditory silence will help you reconnect with your inner voice. The quiet will provide you with an awareness of our society's reliance upon language (and noise), and the multitude of feelings, emotions, and sensory experiences that tend to go neglected because of that reliance.

As a bonus, try this exercise with a partner to experience interpersonal languageless communication. You will likely observe some fascinating and powerful results, and, with practice, will expand your levels of awareness and intimacy as you strengthen your other, non-verbal senses and their abilities to perceive and communicate.[2]

The Singing Two-Step

Mind-Body Sensation ▸ Vocal Manifestation ▸ Language Recognition

Nowhere in the language of vocal technicality have I found a description for the sensation of feeling my whole body engaged in a held tone that seems to dance and resonate throughout my being. Language cannot express the experience of "comfortably influenced freedom" (for lack of a better word-based explanation) that I feel when my voice seems to take on a life of its own, sailing on the air like a kite on a bright, windy day while I stand far below holding the string. Neither have I been able to describe well with words the way waiting air seems to rest pressurized in my chest like a boat perfectly buoyed up on the water—my voice comfortably and harmlessly bobbing in the tides of pitch, volume, and expression.

These sensory, often visual and emotionally charged experiences of singing may seem unrelated to technical and teachable philosophies. But I believe that our languageless experiences, "physical voices," and sixth senses speak to us with great power all the time, providing us with important, powerful glimpses into true technique.

Step One: Mind-Body Sensation ▸ Vocal Manifestation

Many of us are not aware of how to process and utilize what our minds and bodies are subtly trying to relay, however, because we are not paying attention. Just as we speak before we think, we try to "learn how to sing" before taking an inventory of what we already know. Rather than allow our bodies and minds the opportunity to show us what they intuitively understand about singing, we try to help by "breathing deeply" from our "support mechanism," "lengthening" our posture and "reaching" for "notes."

While our intentions are positive, these acts of "assistance and preparation" often cause more harm than good. Trying to implement technique without first considering that you might already be doing it naturally is a bit like taking apart the engine of a car before you have determined that it is not working. First, turn the key. Take the role of objective observer, and let your body and voice show you whether they may already know how to drive.

Step Two: Vocal Manifestation ▸ Language Recognition

Once we have ascertained what our bodies know, the challenge is then to develop a relationship with language that allows us to express and communicate how we sing, without having it interfere with the way we create sound. Words like high, low, bright, rich, breath, straight-tone, vibrato, placement, and support are not inherently problematic, so long as they remain reflections and reminders of the natural and primary physical sensations of singing.

Consider the experiences of standing up, walking, speaking, and tying your shoelaces. No verbal explanation taught you how to do any of these things, yet somehow you figured out how to stand, walk, speak, and tie. Aside from people with physical limitations (and Velcro), I would bet that the world's success rate for these activities is close to 100%.

How did we learn to do these things? Through *observation, imitation, and trial-and-error*. In your mind today, you simply stand up, walk, speak, and tie. However, you will find that trying to explain to someone how to perform these simple tasks is virtually impossible. Thousands of mental and muscular signals and responses occur simultaneously each time we achieve these feats, far too many to monitor and explain sufficiently, efficiently, or effectively with language.

When asked to tie our shoes, walk across the room, or stand for an entrance, the words are simply triggering a process that our bodies engage in automatically. Thus it is meant to be with singing. The commands to increase our volume, shift registers, or round out a tone are not direct orders to manipulate specific musculature. They are meant to trigger the processes that automatically yield these results. Because of our reliance upon language, though, teachers tend to reach for it first ("engage" your diaphragm, "prepare" your throat, "activate" your mask), rather than allow students to begin by experimenting with and experiencing the sensations of how these processes occur naturally. This results in students consciously and physically focusing on isolated actions, thereby halting the integrated, natural functioning of the singing apparatus.

To further complicate the language-first approach, much of the voice-related apparatus has proprioceptive nerve endings,[3] meaning that we cannot readily feel it. How can you engage what you cannot necessarily feel? Elements of the vocal mechanism engage involuntarily as well, breath support being a great case in point. The diaphragm automatically becomes engaged the moment the lungs, on command from the brain, are directed to intake and release air for breathing, speaking, and singing. Though the diaphragm engages only when the lungs inhale or exhale, many people teach that you must consciously and physically prepare and engage your diaphragm before singing. The result is the engaging of a muscle that does not need to be engaged, which inevitably interferes with what the diaphragm knows how to do on its own.

Even if we could consciously and actively engage all the muscles needed to create sound, the body is in a constant state of flux, and the components of the vocal mechanism never feel or behave in entirely the same way. Muscle tone and tensions, colds, mucous, the foods we eat, hydration, stress, fatigue, an awkward night's sleep, adrenaline, and other hormonal levels—not to mention external factors like altitude, allergens, and weather—are always changing, making the sensations of each singing experience throughout the entire body unique. If you sing by first affecting specific elements of your breath, muscles, mouth, or throat, not only will any of a hundred fluctuations throw you off from feeling on track with what you look for in your voice production, your intent will prevent your body from naturally making the subtle modifications and accommodations necessary to sing well.

When you begin with observation, imitation, and trial-and-error, you have the opportunity to first experience the natural functioning of the vocal mechanism. Language may then name, trigger, and explain aspects of the physical experience (walk down the street), and eventually help lead and shape physical-first vocal development and expansion (walk faster down the street, begin to run, now jump in the air).

Neuro-Linguistic Programming (NLP)

> **How we talk to ourselves—the specific words we use—controls the way we think. And the way we think controls how we feel and what we do... Words change the way we feel, and most of us have no conscious awareness of the ones we're using as we communicate with others—and ourselves— daily, much less how they're affecting the way we think and feel moment to moment.[4]**
>
> —Anthony Robbins

Neuro-Linguistic Programming (NLP) is the connection between the words we use and our subsequent belief patterns.[5] Our minds (neuro-) respond to all spoken and unspoken language (linguistic), affecting certain physical and mental responses (programming). Not only the words we speak or think affect us; if they remain unchecked, all verbal and non-verbal societal messages have an influence on how we perceive ourselves and react to others.

The great benefit of NLP is that it can affect as much positive change as it can negative. In her book *Feel the Fear and Do It Anyway*,[6] Susan Jeffers beautifully illustrates the power of NLP and the subconscious through the following example. Push down against someone's arms when they are repeating to themselves "I'm weak" and they will have difficulty lifting them. The downward force you are exerting will likely be greater than the force they can muster to counter. Have them repeat "I'm strong," though, and their physical power changes noticeably, simply by altering the language they are using.

> *Habitually filling your speech with positive thoughts will affect not only your self-perception, but your life as well.*

While you might be skeptical that language can have such a powerful effect on your body, you might be even more surprised to discover the effect it can have on the mind. Regardless of how you may be feeling, one morning this week repeat phrases either out loud or silently such as "I am beautiful/handsome," "I am strong," "I am healthy," "I am kind," "I am loving," "I am powerful," "I am intelligent," and "I am worthy," and note your reaction.

When you fill your mind and speech with positive, self-affirming language rather than complaints, gossip, and self-deprecation, you can and will bring about a change in the way you perceive and feel about yourself. How is this possible if we perhaps do not genuinely feel strong, attractive, powerful, or intelligent? As we discussed in chapter two, our subconscious minds react to what we tell them, regardless of whether or not we consciously believe the messages to be true.

Habitually filling your speech with positive thoughts will affect not only your self-perception, but your life as well. Focus on your strengths rather than your limitations, and you will find that others will do the same. Compliment those you interact with each day, and you will begin to see beauty and kindness in people that you might never have seen before. When someone asks you how you are feeling, consider and share something you truly feel great about or thankful for, and you both will emerge from the interaction with a more positive mindset.

That is not to say that you should ignore pain and frustration or live in denial of them. But when you allow yourself to dwell on your shortcomings or the realities of your life that have yet to become all you have intended or dreamed, you are actually engaging your mental energy to make your situation more permanent. The act and eventual habit of focusing on the positive infuses the challenges, sadness, and suffering in life with hope and inspires action toward that end.

NLP in Singing

Neuro-linguistic programming plays as powerful a role in singing as it does in self-perception, awareness, and actualization. The words that we use to describe our voices, explain the way we sing, and approach learning have a tremendous influence on our physical methodology of sound production. (Imagine how differently you would sing if you never heard the words "engage your diaphragm" and instead, "sing from the bottom of your soul.")

Consider what happens when someone, whether a professional singer or not, is asked to perform. While virtually no one gives a thought to the process of speaking (except public speaking), someone asking us to sing often triggers some or all of the following internal or verbal responses:

- I'm not prepared.
- I'm not in good voice today.
- I am unable to sing this song well.
- What if I don't sound good?
- What if I crack, or mess up?
- Will people like the way I sound?
- I'm going to make a fool of myself.
- I am so nervous.

The body hears and believes the mind, and prepares to defend itself against an onslaught of potential negative results and imaginary judgment. Muscles tighten, breathing becomes affected, and the performance suffers.

Whether you are unsure of yourself as a singer, have a voice riddled with tension, or are terrified of performing, you can begin to alter your relationship with your voice simply by altering the language you use to refer to it. Tell yourself:

- My voice is powerful.
- My voice is beautiful.
- My voice and I have a great relationship.
- My voice works effortlessly and on command.
- My voice is comfortable and healthy.[7]
- My voice is a gift that I want to share with others.
- All ranges are easy for me.
- All styles of singing are easy.

And so on. It may seem silly or impossible that repeating certain phrases can alter and improve the way you sing, but give it a try. What you will discover is that many of the problems we all have with our voices have less to do with our actual instruments, and more to do with the way we perceive, approach, and speak about them—and ourselves. Positive language will instruct the body and mind to trust and relax, and the voice will at last have a fighting chance.

Putting NLP to the Test

"I really want to sing this song, but the highest note, a C-sharp, is too high for me."

Two red flags went up when a client uttered this seemingly harmless sentence in a session: one for the use of the word "high," and the other for the naming of a specific note. Many sessions contain potential language pollution like this, which serves to keep the walls tall and strong around otherwise beautiful, healthy voices.

As we have discussed, our minds and bodies are notorious for believing what we tell them. When we hear the word "high," our minds set in motion a parade of thoughts and mental pictures associated with this familiar term. We mentally connect it to up, unreachable, tall, vertical, and every other word that implies somewhere above where we are now. With this NLP relationship, it is no wonder that singers tend to stretch upward with their energy, breath, bodies, throats, and even eyebrows to hit high notes.[8]

In reality, there is no such thing as a high note. The vocal folds, resting in the larynx, move horizontally, vibrating faster for higher notes, and slower for lower notes, much like the strings on a guitar. There is never a need to reach (which implies a straining movement) up or down, to hit a note.

Where did this prevalent tendency come from, then? From assigning a word unrelated to the reality of the physical process. My clients who have trouble hitting "high" notes have no problem screaming "What's up?!" when they walk into a session, totally oblivious to the fact that their voices just sailed five to ten notes past those they swear cause them so much frustration when singing.

Our minds and bodies are notorious for believing what we tell them.

The same NLP pitfalls hold true for the names we assign to notes. What initially served to simplify and encourage uniformity of notation and communication among musicians has become, in many ways, a great limitation. The client from the above example had decided that a B-natural above middle C was the highest note she could reach, and that she was unable to hit any note higher than that.

This conclusion was not based in reality. The experience of a C-sharp, or any note for that matter, is completely different in every song, depending on a host of variables. The style of the song, the register we use, the notes that precede it and the notes that follow it, the text that is sung on the note and preceding notes, and our ability to modify vowels can all change the way a specific note is experienced. A note that might be perfectly comfortable in a person's range often becomes terribly hard when it is the high point of a piece. The brain is so accustomed to soaring choruses that emotionally peak (another "up" word) on a high note, that the body thinks it needs to reach with the voice as well as with the emotion.

Musical notation visually perpetuates this up-and-down relationship by placing higher notes graphically above lower ones on the page. Instead, look at the piano as a more useful metaphor for the voice box. There is no high and low in the up-and-down sense, as every note lies on the same plane. There are no notes that are harder for the fingers to reach than others, as a simple lateral move with the hand and arm results in effortlessly playing any note on the instrument, just as your air and musculature adjust slightly to approach different pitches when singing.

To prove this to my disbelieving clients (who honestly believe it is the note that is hard for them), I play the piece we are working on a whole- or half-step lower without telling them, and they inevitably still have trouble reaching the highest note—a note they had been singing elsewhere in the song's original key without any difficulty.

Using this exercise with my clients with perfect pitch is virtually impossible, as their ears tell them right away that I am cheating. Most of these clients have already decided and defined in advance which pitches are hard for them to hit, and therefore get nervous and tense on their approach to whatever notes they have pre-designated as difficult in any and every song. ("Approach" is a word I like, because it paints a picture of driving along a horizontal path toward a home, as opposed to going "up" to a note.) For these clients, a series of exercises using vocal sliding can help break the mind blocks that they have built up around specific notes, as the movement is so rapid that the mind cannot readily distinguish and define pitch values.[9]

I myself had a problem with pitch definition. Years ago, I observed that B-flat above middle C was the last (as opposed to "highest") note I could comfortably produce (as opposed to "hit") in my chest range before my voice desired to shift (as opposed to "had to shift") into my falsetto (as opposed to "head voice," as the head is "higher" than the chest). While I believed that I had retained an open mind about this issue, I was one day shocked to find myself effortlessly and comfortably singing a D-natural in my chest voice (four half-steps higher) in a recording session. I was not even aware that it happened, but when it was pointed out to me, I realized that I had been allowing my preconceived notions to limit my relationship with an ever-changing voice in ever-changing circumstances. I had been allowing language to define and limit my experience of singing, rather than remain a reflection of the actual process.

Take time to consider whether the words you use and notions you subscribe to are helping to free or hinder your singing.

Language is not the problem. Our relationship with language is what often gets us into trouble. Today, I can use words like "high" and "reach" and name pitches without triggering the common reactions we have discussed here. But in order to do that, I first had to understand what my voice and body were doing physically, and then choose words to communicate and describe the process, rather than control and dictate it.

Take time to consider whether the words you use and notions you subscribe to are helping to free or hinder your singing. Then create and implement language that reflects and expresses the physical process as you experience it. A world of mental blocks and physical tensions will dissipate, as you uncover—recover—a much healthier and more enjoyable process of singing and learning to sing.

Chapter 4

Learning

A combination of factors—including personality, brain structure, nature, and conditioning—dictates the way we best process and internalize information. As no two people or life experiences are the same, each of us has our own unique way of seeing the world and understanding all that is in it.

While some students have the privilege of education and tutoring targeted to their specific needs and preferences, most find themselves immersed in a system of education that cannot possibly be ideal, or even adequate, for everyone. The result is that the majority of people are inappropriately qualified for the education they receive, and thereby inadequately prepared for the world in which they later find themselves.

Getting Started on the Wrong Foot

> **As knowledge becomes increasingly clever, versatile, and artful, the people all around… struggle to grasp what they do not know, but make no attempt to grasp what they know already. From this, more confusion comes.[1]**
>
> —Chuang Tse

While I have been fortunate over the years to discover how I learn best, this knowledge did not come easily. As a child, I worked hard and did my best to impress my teachers and to succeed in the work they assigned me. When I got good grades, I perceived myself as intelligent. When I had trouble with math and science, I felt my confidence in my intelligence wane. Convinced that any lack of understanding was the result of insufficient studying or attention on my part, I was at my desk late into the night, working to memorize all I could about chemistry and calculus. I kept trying harder rather than considering that a *smarter* approach might be necessary, or even possible.

I have since discovered that the purpose of education is not memorization or the acquisition of facts and information. In fact, quite the opposite is true in learning, life, and certainly singing. Regardless of the subject, the specific information is not the destination, but the means to the larger destination of understanding. Facts and certain knowledge are the convenient byproducts of awareness and wonder. When you focus on the goal, namely, the process of learning, facts and details are more easily absorbed.

Regardless of the subject, the specific information is not the destination, but the means to the larger destination of understanding.

My mother is a living example of this principle. Not only can she discuss facts relating to most world events, past or present, she seems to have a thorough and effortless understanding of virtually every subject. A "walking encyclopedia" is a description that suits her well.

In speaking with her today, the reality becomes clear. While she is certainly an intelligent woman, it is not genius that enables her to comprehend and retain so much information. She simply loves to learn, and always has. She recalls the good fortune of having teachers who encouraged the love of learning in their students by placing emphasis on enthusiasm rather than memorization, on curiosity rather than grades. Teachers presented topics as living and breathing concepts for the children to appreciate and process in their own ways, rather than as intangible facts that bore little relevance to their lives. Going to school for her was therefore a joy, and learning was fully integrated and easily retained.

While I was taught a vast amount of information in school, I never really learned how to learn. Unlike my mother's experience, mine did not revolve around true comprehension. Instructors gave grades based—as they often still are—on yes/no, right/wrong exams that tested the ability to memorize and regurgitate facts, rather than the ability to reason or think abstractly. Not having a way to connect personally and meaningfully to the information, I studied the facts as hard as I could, from the outside looking in.

Sadly, when the cramming of details to determine "mastery" supersedes curiosity, contemplation, and connection, people rarely learn or retain anything of value. Many children find ways to do well with this style of instruction by becoming masterful at the art of short-term memorization or managing to develop meaning within the confines of fact absorption. Unfortunately, many more find themselves bored, confused, angry or worse… incorrectly branded as unintelligent, difficult, or even learning disabled.

A Look at John

After college, I spent a year working with five- to ten-year-olds in a private school environment. While it was a joy to be around the kids, it was painful to watch many of them getting more and more lost in a system of learning that did not make sense.

One student in particular had a tremendous amount of trouble. I met him when he was nine years old, in the beginning of his fourth grade year, two years after the school labeled him a possibly learning-disabled child with a disastrous behavior and scholastic record. Despite the school's warnings, I thoroughly enjoyed my time with John. While the conventions of academics had given him trouble, he was enormously intuitive and bright, with a remarkable talent for the violin at such a young age.

I watched him go through each school day, unable to handle the cursory brushing over of information. He wanted to delve deeply into each topic and stay there until he had had his fill. When he would arrive to my classroom, he was still lost in the questions and mental pictures of the last class. By the time he had managed to climb out of that pool of knowledge, we were already halfway through our lesson. Frustrated, he would give up and return again and again to being discouraged and difficult—hurt by the teasing of the other students and crushed by being labeled unintelligent by the staff. Thus, the door began to close on the positive sense of self necessary to allow him to flourish as a musician, a student, and a person.

Like so many students, John's inherent preference for a more creative and in-depth approach to learning was overlooked by a system geared toward measuring achievement based more on grades than on comprehension. I believed John's behavior problems to be a product of frustration and boredom rather than ADD or ADHD, however, and was eager to test my theory.[2]

We spent the semester playing a little game. I informed the students that the grades for the first month would be based on class participation rather than tests. The result? Hands shot up in the air, but responses consisted of more fluff than substance. The kids, John included, were trying desperately to do whatever they thought they had to do to get the grade, even at the age of nine.

The next month, I told them that we were there just to have fun, and to forget about grades completely. If we learned, great. It not, fine. The results were amazing. After an initial few days of playful—then tentative— rambunctiousness, everyone relaxed. The kids each worked at their own pace, asked questions without embarrassment, were kinder to one another, and learned more. We continued the experiment through the end of the year, in which time everyone thrived, especially John.

Getting Back on Track

That is what learning is. You suddenly understand something you've understood all your life, but in a new way.[3]

—Doris Lessing

By the time I reached high school, I truly believed that I was terrible at math. My grades were actually OK, but I was convinced that I simply was not hardwired for algebra and calculus. I was great in English, writing, history, literature, music—all of the humanities—so I found myself buying into the "people are good at either languages and art or math and science" mentality. My thoughts turned into reality (as they usually do) and I hated math and science, subconsciously conditioning myself for failure. I would become frustrated when I could not grasp a concept, then panic as the rest of the class moved on. Terrified that I would be left behind, I attacked the subjects (particularly math) in a frenzy. Long nights of memorization and cramming resulted in good grades, but I never thoroughly understood or comprehended the material.

Interestingly, when I studied for the Graduate Record Examination (GRE) years later, the same material that gave me so much trouble in high school became effortlessly acquired knowledge. It had not gotten any easier, and I had not retained much from school. It was a shift in my mentality and outlook on learning that made the topics much more accessible. Between my horrible experience with high school math and the time I took the GRE, I had learned how to learn, thus altering my attitude toward math and other "difficult" subjects.

I was able to approach math with the same mindset as I do literature and the humanities, and my enjoyment and retention soared.

It turns out that calculus and chemistry are not inherently problematic for me. However, because I was introduced to them in high school as technical facts and equations with nothing for me to connect to visually or conceptually, I was lost. As an adult, I recognized that my mind is more creative than technical in certain ways, and I used this wisdom to my advantage. By replacing my old learning patterns and frustration with a more positive, creative—and fearless—method of information acquisition, I was able to approach math with the same mindset as I do literature and the humanities, and my enjoyment and retention soared.

Learning How to Learn

Though it took me some time to work out, learning how to learn is actually a rather simple process—one you most likely have a good grasp of, even if you are unaware of it. Take the words "learning" and "education" out of the equation (take out the word "equation," as well!) and what are you looking at? Remove all negative associations you might have with the education process—language and otherwise— and simply consider the way you see the world and yourself in it. The picture then becomes clearer.

Understanding Yourself

What are you passionate about? What do your relationships with friends and family look like? What are the things you like and/or dislike about the work you do? Do you prefer to be around lots of people or to be by yourself? Are you a pensive person who enjoys deep analysis, or do you find yourself restless when alone and in silence for long periods of time? Do you tend to be more creative or more technical in the way you think?[4]

Are you a visual learner or an aural learner, or both? Do you gravitate toward facts or toward concepts? Are you a morning person or an evening person? Do you prefer to work endlessly at a task until it is completed, or to approach projects and activities in stages? Are you good with a time-oriented schedule, or does the clock irritate you when focused on a project?

How do music, lighting, and other external stimuli affect your ability to process and retain information? Are you easily distracted? Are you comfortable being indoors for long periods of time, or do you need to have contact with nature and the sun in order to feel productive and happy?

In the answers to these and similar questions lie not only how you prefer to relate to the world and others, but how you learn best. Imagine the potential for tremendous growth… or stagnation. If your mind functions optimally at night, waking up at 7 a.m. to go to work or school will not enable you to be your best. If you thrive on brainstorming with others and relish their feedback, you will not do well with an isolated online MBA program. If you are a visual or hands-on learner, listening to a litany of facts in a lecture will not only leave you distracted and bored, it will likely rob you of your interest in the subject.

Yet, these scenarios are prevalent, particularly in our schools. The same child that will avoid reading ten pages of a homework assignment will stay up all night reading Harry Potter or working on the computer.[5] This is not necessarily a sign of immaturity or a lack of commitment to education. This is simply an individual who is attracted to enjoyable and relevant information, presented at a time and in an environment best suited to that individual.

Granted, some required subjects are not as thrilling as others, and it is certainly important to learn how to be flexible. But what teenagers would not want to understand finance and the stock market if they saw that these subjects related to the potential increase of disposable income? What kids would not enjoy reading more if the material were relevant to their lives and dreams? The creators of popular children's television shows, books, and games spend a lot of time, money, and energy learning about what attracts and retains kids' attention. How can our schools begin to compete and truly educate when this information rarely influences the design of their curriculums?

If the understanding of our personal preferences is so essential to successful learning, why do so few of us think about and apply these principles once we are out on our own? Again, we tend to bring our conditioning forward from childhood to adulthood without questioning whether it has been working for us. With most of us trained to think that learning on any level is only about taking in the information presented in the way that it is presented and no one teaching us otherwise, we have little reason to reconsider our submissive role in the process.

For a long time, I did not consider that my personality and preferences could influence and even enhance my learning, and, eventually, my working environment. On many levels, I had learned to think that it was my job to fit myself into the world, with my success being determined by how well I "succeeded" as measured by societal approval and, eventually, money, rather than by what I was truly learning and contributing—a variation on the familiar theme of my early education experience.

There is a world of endless opportunity for the creating out there if we are willing to take our lives out of automatic pilot and consider who it is we really are.

They say hindsight is 20/20, and it is now clear to me how important it is to get past this notion. I promise you, if my happiness and success were contingent upon a nine-to-five technical job in an isolated, windowless cubicle, I would fail at both miserably. It is not in my make-up to work in that type of environment, with that type of information, on that type of schedule. Fortunately, there is a world of endless opportunity for the creating out there if we are willing to take our lives out of automatic pilot and consider who it is we really are, what it is we really want to do, and how we should best go about getting there.

Self-Awareness, Self-Guided Learning, and Life-Long Self-Directed Education

Once you have a firm grasp of your best learning practices, you must then put them into action by taking responsibility for your own learning. This not only means having a stake in what, how, where, and when you will learn, but learning to collaborate with your educators.

When working with a teacher, hiring a therapist, or consulting a coach, you are employing them to help you grow in a certain area of understanding.

This turns the standard model of education on its head, as most of us believe that the balance of power in the teacher-student relationship is heavily in favor of the teacher. From the time we begin school, teachers are forced to take on the role of disciplinarian, above and beyond their teaching duties. These roles are intermingled over time, and 12-plus years of conditioning result in most of us associating the position of teacher with power, discipline, and authority.

Look carefully at these relationships, though. The balance of power is actually in your favor! When working with a teacher, hiring a therapist, or consulting a coach, *you* are employing *them* to help you grow in a certain area of understanding. They are auditioning for you, so to speak, and need to convince you that they are qualified to provide you with the service that you want.

While it might be difficult for a ten-year-old to demand a healthy, co-learning relationship with a fifth grade teacher, it is not unreasonable for you to do so as an adult. Still, many people perpetuate the powerless state that frequently characterizes the student position when it comes to relationships with therapists, counselors, and coaches, as well as doctors, lawyers, and other specialists.

Getting Back on Track Vocally

We should treat our minds, that is, ourselves, as innocent and ingenious children, whose guardians we are, and be careful what objects and what subjects we thrust on their attention.[6]

—Henry David Thoreau

Summer came to me after working for two years with a coach in preparation for recording her first major label CD. An R&B singer with a gorgeous voice, she was also a voice teacher herself. Still, her years of experience and solid grasp of vocal production did not prevent her from jumping headfirst into an unhealthy, co-dependent relationship with another coach.

Even the most open-minded and nurturing coaches cannot properly help you if you do not bring the right mindset to the table.

Not only was Summer told that she could not perform a show without first seeing her teacher, she was forbidden from singing or recording any song without first rehearsing it with her to ensure she would not "hurt herself." In a very short time, the predictable effects of this relationship had taken their toll on Summer's voice and mind. She was so terrified of singing incorrectly that all of the emotion and freedom were gone from her voice, squeezed out by fear and over-thinking.

A few sessions together cleared up a large portion of the psychological nonsense that Summer had taken on, at which point I asked her why she had allowed herself to become involved in such an unhealthy situation. Her response was all too familiar: Despite confusion, lack of progress and discomfort, Summer assumed the coach knew what was best. And while she eventually had the courage to leave, a sense of guilt remained that the unsuccessful experience had somehow been her fault.

Without having redefined the way we learn from childhood, many of us slip back into the unhealthy aspects of the teacher and student roles that are not ideal in a coaching relationship—or any relationship. A lack of confidence, a desire to impress, the pressure to succeed, a fear of failing… these feelings do not serve to set the stage for an advantageous experience. Even the most open-minded and nurturing coaches cannot properly help you if you do not bring the right mindset to the table.

Learning, in every context, is a give-and-take arrangement—a dance, if you will. You lead, now he leads. She leads, now you lead. The back and forth, not only of the specific information, but also of the experiences and perspectives you each have are key in helping to bring that information to life. This dance does not require the act of unhealthy submission. It requires the desire of both parties to fully partner, respect, and learn with open minds.

A coach might know more about technique than you, but that does not mean that he or she knows how to communicate that information in a way that makes sense to you. If you feel discomfort or do not understand what your coach is trying to explain, do not automatically doubt yourself, regardless of how talented, famous, or experienced he or she is. Ask to have the information explained in a new way or to try a new approach. See if you can come up with a common vision for growing your voice that makes the most sense to you. If your coach is uninterested in co-learning, co-discovery, and co-creating an ideal way for you to learn, leave.

Becoming the Teacher

The extraordinary thing about life is that each of us sees the world differently, and there are many "right ways" to do things.[7]

–John Paul Schaefer

One of the most important discoveries I have made about singing is that there is no such thing as one correct technique—at least not in a teachable, tangible sense. While every person in a 100-member choir might be physically producing sound the same way, they are each having a wholly unique experience of that process. Only by first focusing on, trusting, and understanding that experience can any understanding of technique leap off the textbook pages and come to life with personal meaning.

Truth #4: *You Are Your Best Teacher*

If I tell you how it feels when I sing a note correctly in an effort to teach you how to do the same, I am making some potentially dangerous and very likely false assumptions. First, I am assuming that we feel the same things when creating sound. I am also assuming that you will be able to connect to my verbal and/or metaphorical explanations of how singing feels to me. Finally, I am assuming that we learn and process information in the same way, and that we translate our feelings into language in the same way—and in all of this, assuming that you are even a language-oriented person!

In an effort to be helpful, many coaches actually detract from their clients' learning by first relating the process of singing as they understand it. This can include, as in Summer's case, the projecting of a coach's own fears and insecurities—vocal and otherwise—onto the client.

Stephen Covey's "Seek first to understand, then to be understood" is an apt motto for any coach.[8] It is the student, rather than the teacher, who holds the key to unlocking the voice. In order to help you learn, it is imperative that a coach first observe you, listen to you, and garner all the information possible about you. With no one forcing you to adopt the coach's version of what correct singing should feel like, you are able to explore how you best experience the process of singing.

Carolyn and Marty

Carolyn describes the sensation of breath support as, "My tummy is singing." Marty calls his speech-like singing "spinging," which helps him remember that correct singing is really very similar to speaking. I have my own set of metaphors and mental links that help me to relax and sing freely, and while Carolyn understands some of them, "spinging" makes no sense to her. Nothing makes sense to Marty except "spinging."

It is the student, rather than the teacher, who holds the key to unlocking the voice.

I began working with Carolyn and Marty at about the same time. As with all of my clients, I observed and tried to understand the different ways they approached singing and learning. I gave them permission to experiment with their voices, constantly watching how they handled their relationships with success, frustration, and their instruments. I listened to their histories, both personal and musical, and assessed how these experiences affected their singing.

I monitored their attention spans, energy levels, and their ability to manage practice and discipline. I listened to and learned their verbal and non-verbal vocal languages, and found ways to guide and train them in a manner that made them feel empowered.

While I took the same approach with Carolyn and Marty, their lessons look and feel entirely different. Marty comes in the morning when his brain is most alert and active, and I visit Carolyn's studio in the afternoon, where and when she feels more grounded and comfortable. Marty needs to talk about what he has learned for a good 15 minutes before we sing a note, whereas Carolyn is already singing when I walk in. Marty does best with exercises after we have worked on songs, as his passion for the music helps him connect to his best voice, while Carolyn likes the ritual of the vocalise first.

Marty is very creative; Carolyn is very technical. Marty likes bright lights and opened windows; Carolyn has candles and incense burning in her little cave. Marty needs, and even likes, to be pushed at times, whereas Carolyn is better served discovering things for herself, regardless of how long it may take her. Marty wants to be taught; Carolyn requires partnership. Marty is hyperactive; Carolyn is mellow. Marty and I do a lot of talking; Carolyn learns best through non-verbal communication. Marty is playful; Carolyn is emotional.

As different as their sessions are, the destination remains the same: healthy singing, healthy mindset, healthy life. Having the space and permission to seek out and apply their personal-best approaches to their voices and themselves, both Carolyn and Marty have thrived.

While I am the one technically in charge of the sessions, I am following their leads. They are teaching me how to teach them. In time, this dynamic can expand to incredibly powerful levels. Once trust and a sense of true camaraderie are born, the dance is much smoother, more complex, and more beautiful. Learning increases exponentially.

Finding the Right Partner

Vocal training requires you to bare not only your voice, but also your heart and even your soul to another; that is, to become truly vulnerable. Therefore, it is imperative to have a sense of confidence about both who you are and what you already know when looking for a coach. Remember that you come to the table with a great amount of knowledge about your voice and how you relate to it from a lifetime of hands-on experience.

Even the best coaches have their limitations.

Also important, and often overlooked, is to know what it is you hope to achieve. Do you want to heal an existing vocal problem, craft a style for yourself, or maintain and develop an already healthy voice? Do you want someone who will casually help you explore your potential, or do you need to be ready to perform an important gig by early next week? There is a big difference between wanting to strengthen your instrument and wanting to repair muscle damage and mis-education, between preparing for an impending tour and coming out of a vocal hibernation. There is a big difference between a technician and a stylistic coach. Does the person you are considering specialize in your area of music? Studying with an opera singer if you want a career in the pop world (or vice versa) might not do you much good, unless that teacher is enormously versatile and open-minded.

Even the best coaches have their limitations, and the truly great ones will let know what they do and do not specialize in, as well as if and when the time has come for you to move on. It is also very important to find someone who does not want you to sound like them, and who will make sure that you do not start to change your own sound as a conscious or unconscious result of working together and observing them sing. It is possible to learn from a coach—or any singer—via imitation without it affecting how you create sound and your own particular style.

Whatever your specific goals, in my opinion, the best teachers are those who approach the voice, music, and life with humility and curiosity—those who want to learn as much as they want to teach. Look for someone who is eager for you to discover and celebrate your strengths and weaknesses, because knowing what not to do is often as important as knowing what to do.

The process of learning and discovery should be exciting rather than frustrating, and certainly not stagnant. I had a client come to me just last week from a coach who told her that learning to sing healthily would take her five years! Not so. If you have been working on anything for six months with no improvement or increased understanding, it may be time to try a new teacher, or certainly a new approach.

> *Whatever your specific goals, the best teachers are those who approach the voice, music, and life with humility and curiosity.*

Understanding Time: Redefining Your Experience

With that said, patience is necessary, even with the right coach. Most of us enter the learning process with a specific goal in mind that we intend to achieve in a certain fashion, in a certain amount of time. When we do not meet that goal how or when we envisioned it happening, we become frustrated. I watch many of my clients' irritations build when they do not learn and internalize concepts as quickly as they would like.

It has taken you a lifetime to develop your physical and mental bad habits, so how can you expect to undo them in ten minutes? Taking ten weeks or even ten months to see things in a new way, shift your perspective, and develop a new set of habits is a worthwhile investment if your goal is a life-long relationship with your instrument.

Our impatience is not only about not wanting to fail. It has to do with not enjoying and appreciating the process of learning. It comes from believing that singing—like life—is a project with a measurable goal, rather than an experience and a journey. This attitude, incidentally, serves to lengthen the process.

If you want a quick fix, I can give you some tricks to avoid fatigue and improve your performance for your show tomorrow night. But what about the next 150 shows? Instead, why not make the conscious choice to figure out how you learn best and embrace the process as an ongoing, every day experience? I am not saying you cannot have measurable vocal goals, or that you should feel blissfully unconcerned with what your critics have to say. But I am telling you that the more you approach your voice—and yourself—with wonder, patience, and care, the more predictable and powerful results you will achieve.

Chapter 5

The Brain in Singing

We have spent the last few chapters learning about the variety of ways people think, communicate, and learn. Now, let's take a look at why these differences exist and how they affect our singing—answers that lie in the magnificent mass we call the brain and in our conscious and unconscious realities that are housed there.

The Right and Left Hemispheres

The brain is divided into two separate hemispheres, which act alone and together to process and internalize information. A channel-like connection called the *corpus callosum* links them, streaming an endless amount of data back and forth between the two.

Unlike most of the animal kingdom, our two hemispheres are not mirror images of one another. The left hemisphere (which controls the right side of the body) is considered the dominant hemisphere, and the right (which controls the left side), the non-dominant.[1] Despite their proximity to each other and their partnership in our daily functioning, they "think" completely differently in terms of how they process and respond to information.

Areas of both sides of the brain work together to yield functioning of technical and creative natures.

For decades, the common language used by both teachers and students of creativity has been that of the right brain and the left brain. This model is based upon the idea that the left, or dominant hemisphere, is responsible for the technical, language-based, and time-bound functioning of the mind, with the right, non-dominant hemisphere responsible for creativity, music, and art. In certain aspects, this distinction is true. For example, the technical aspects of speech (grammar, syntax, and vocabulary) are indeed largely processed in the areas of the left hemisphere, while the musical aspects of speech (the "melody" of the spoken voice) and early musical perception itself are processed primarily in the right.

The science, however, is actually far more complex. To begin, the classifications of "creative" and "technical" that have been attributed to the right and left hemispheres, respectively, are not exclusively so. There are various areas of the left hemisphere that encourage creativity, as well as areas of the right hemisphere that deal with language and a sense of time. In addition, studies have shown that the same information can be processed by two different people in two different hemispheres. For example, while music is generally processed in large part in the right hemisphere, many professional musicians have been shown to process music predominantly in the left. Finally, more often than not, areas of both sides of the brain work together to yield functioning of technical and creative natures.[2]

In the face of the more intricate physiology, the right and left brain model is certainly convenient for simplifying the workings of the mind. But a more correct view focuses less on *where* information is processed, and more on *how* that information manifests in thoughts and behavior. Therefore, most of my discussion will use the terms "the technical mind" and "the creative mind," rather than the traditional right- and left-brain model.

Characteristics Commonly Attributed to the Right and Left Hemispheres

Technical (Left/Dominant Hemisphere)	Creative (Right/Non-Dominant Hemisphere)
Thinking	Feeling
Memorization-based learning	Comprehension-based learning
Time-bound, systematic structure	Timeless, unstructured immersion
Analytical	Observational
Language-based understanding	Language-less, sensory comprehension
Ego-based	Pleasure-based
Concrete	Abstract
Desires to be right or wrong	Uninterested in validation
Competitive	Non-competitive
Outcome-oriented	Experience-oriented
Methodical and reasoning	Instinctive and intuitive
Black and white	Grey

While some people relate to aspects of both columns, most people I know find themselves primarily depicted by traits in one of the two.[3]

If you feel better represented by the first column, you are more technical in your approach to life and learning. Lawyers, accountants, engineers, and surgeons tend to be very technical. There is not a lot of room for grey in this world, and even less for a perceived failure. Success is a function of arriving at a predetermined goal, rather than a process to enjoy.

Outcome-oriented and time-structured, the technically minded crave concrete answers to all questions and challenges, and prefer that those answers can be written down and explained in a black-and-white manner. Either it will work, or it won't. Either it will sell, or it won't. Theoretical knowledge requiring "faith" in lieu of certain evidence or logic is unattractive without tangible data—real or invented.

The technically minded crave concrete answers to all questions and challenges, and prefer that those answers can be written down and explained in a black-and-white manner.

Technically minded people prefer to have things organized, at least in the mind, which seldom rests from thoughts and chatter. While incessant thinking helps them "get the job done right" through strategic reasoning, it is very hard to get the brain to stop and to experience life in the moment—for instance, to revel in the colors of a sunset or listen long to the sounds of the world around them. If it is not in their day planners, they are not likely to have time for it, thereby missing a multitude of unplanned and sensory experiences that await the more creative observer.

Even when the technically minded have a strong creative side, they have difficulty nurturing that creativity in themselves and others unless they can see some predictable or timely gain—financial, career, ego, or otherwise. While this may keep them in a nice car and house, they are inclined to become out-of-touch with the creativity and dreams they have likely neglected in order to achieve "success," resulting in feelings of stress and/or lack of fulfillment. In addition, while their technical nature might have been the key to getting that great corporate job, their preference for seeing everything in black and white may prevent them from taking chances and discovering out-of-the-box ideas that come more easily to their creative contemporaries.

Creatively minded individuals seek the corners of grey for every bit of knowledge that lies between black and white, measuring success by the trinkets of wisdom gained along the journey.

If this does not sound like you, you may identify more clearly with the second column, where philosophy, poetry, art, design, and other creative pursuits reign supreme. Creatively minded individuals seek the corners of grey for every bit of knowledge that lies between black and white, measuring success by the trinkets of wisdom gained along the journey, rather than by the arrival at a prescribed destination. Like walking through the woods, they will decide which paths to take based not on where they allegedly lead, but on which ones look the most interesting at the time. Faith, intuition, and energy-perception—rather than technical explanations and facts—are more convincing evidence for the creative mind, while truths and theories mean nothing if the creative individual cannot experience the information in a tangible way.

Sometimes dwelling on one subject for an extended time, other times darting from topic to topic, the creatively minded always dive deeply into the essence of what they are doing. While no one necessarily enjoys busy work, they are hopelessly bored by it and have difficulty performing any task that lacks meaning and purpose.

Generally uninterested in time structure, creatively minded individuals wait until the mood to work strikes, which could mean zoning out for a few days and then jumping headfirst into an activity, or staying up all night to pursue an idea. Organization is overrated; their creativity is not contingent upon an immaculate working environment.

While creatively minded people in many ways enjoy a richer and more colorful life, their passion and single-minded concern for the experience can cause great difficulty. Often, they are so lost in creative pursuits that they overlook things such as scheduling and paying the bills, not to mention sleeping and eating. The world misinterprets this as laziness, disorganization, or apathy, traits that generally are not accurate descriptions of their true character.

Unless blessed with a family or community that appreciates and supports an artistic nature, the creatively minded are in for a tough ride. Consider how our culture values a painter as compared to a lawyer, a musician as compared to a doctor. While society loves to highlight and admire the many brilliant creative manifestations of this type (at least the successful ones), it is less likely to financially compensate others for what it perceives as "hobbies." Many artists I know and work with feel a perpetual sense of devaluation by society for their artistic pursuits, encouraged instead to believe that a time-rigid, corporate, and predictable existence is best. When creative minds subscribe to this prevalent mentality and try to conform to the corporate model to earn a living, boredom and frustration often follow as they fight their true creative nature. This will not only take a toll on creativity, but on self-confidence as well.

Either/Or Thinking

It is true that most people have a natural preference either for technical thinking or creative thinking, but it is just that—a preference.

So, which is better: to be creative or to be technical? While both have their strengths, neither is—nor can be—adequate in providing all the tools necessary to fully experience and participate in life, as we have just seen. Even the most specific creative and technical activities require the skill sets of both for optimal outcomes. For example, great singing and performing require a high degree of creative energy, but music theory is extremely technical. Therefore, the best musicians are able to access both skill sets on command.[4]

If most of us tend to be either one or the other, however, does that mean we are stuck with only half the skills necessary to live an optimal life? Not at all. It is true that most people have a natural preference for and better relate to one of the two previous descriptions, but it is just that—a preference—the power of which depends on how you preceive and define the word. (NLP once again!) If you decide to define your preference as "the only feasible and advantageous option available," you will persist in believing that you are either creative or technical, shutting the door on valuable mental resources that, while perhaps underdeveloped, are certainly not non-existent. However, if you believe that a preference is the way you prefer and decide to do something, you move from being a victim of conditioning to a nurturer of potential and a creator of reality—a reality in which the mind works to expand and improve your experience of living, thinking, and working, as well as singing.

Still, the vast majority of us persist in what I call either/or thinking. We are creative or technical, good at math or music, talented in art or business. From a very early age, most of us decide—consciously and unconsciously—that we are one or the other, exclusively develop the traits attributed to that end, and neglect the rest because we have:

- "discovered" the way we think "best," and never consider any other way of doing so.
- "discovered" the way we think "best," and believe that we're unable to think optimally in any other way.
- "discovered" the way we think "best," and don't believe that it is possible to develop a new way of thinking without somehow detracting from the power and strength of the former.

Believing that our experiences reflect the full extent of our potential, we persist in either/or thinking rather than tap into the full resources of our minds. Why? For the same reason I allowed chemistry and calculus to intimidate me for so long, for the same reasons we limit ourselves in so many areas—because of conditioning and the reliance upon scarcity-based thinking.

Conditioning

Our brains are designed to effortlessly call upon whatever skill sets are required for various situations. Yet, many factors conspire to change and distort this natural, whole-brain intelligence.

Young children are little hedonists running wild in the world. Seeing, touching, tasting, smelling, and listening to everything around them, they observe and internalize in a sensory way. With nothing to qualify or quantify, their information is wholly processed through observation and stored as such in their unconscious knowing.[5]

Between the ages of two and three, however, this process is interrupted, as we touched upon in the second chapter. Two specific areas of the brain start to develop that begin to inhibit this sensory experience by introducing the ability to categorize information in a factual and time-oriented way, and to judge it based on societal and moral norms.[6]

These inhibitors are not inherently detrimental to creativity, as they allow us to organize facts, information, and memories, and to understand and comply with behavioral and societal standards. However, by the time children learn to speak, these inhibitors are overly empowered by our culture's technically oriented approaches to language, scheduling, and functioning. The entrance into our structured education system further places these technical inhibitors into a powerful, central, long-term role. The intuitive, creative mind is remanded to the shadows where it waits patiently for its turn to shine.[7]

Unfortunately, that turn rarely comes. With increasing demands upon the technical skill set, we fall more and more out of practice and out of touch with the experience of intuitive creativity. When (or if) creativity is called for, the technical mind has no choice but to try its hand, because it has been convinced that it can and should handle anything that comes its way. The results are inevitably disappointing, for true creative success is virtually impossible when the inhibitors are in charge. No longer certain of how to tap into our creativity, a few botched attempts by the technical mind are all it takes for us to incorrectly assume that we are "just not good" at music and art.

This mentality goes both ways. Children gifted in art, music, and abstract thought tend to have great difficulty when introduced to society's technical and time-bound approaches to life and learning, and choose to stay in their creative and sensory-rich comfort zones instead. While this helps their artistic ability and sense of self to thrive, many (including John from the previous chapter) eventually give up rather than continue to struggle in an unfamiliar system of thought where they repeatedly fail.

Scarcity vs. Abundance

Janice began composing and painting at a very young age, and continues to excel in music and art. Like many highly creative people, teachers classified her as gifted in early childhood, though her schoolwork did not reflect her brilliance. Rather than try to keep up in an education system that made little sense to her, she turned repeatedly to what she could succeed in—her art and music.

What we stand to gain oftentimes far outweighs what we spend and give away.

In conversing with her today at the age of 28, two things are clear. While she is very creative and very gifted, she is terrified of anything that is remotely technical. Her conviction that she lacks an affinity for the methodic is evident in her language, behavior, and perception of reality. Terrible with scheduling, money, organization, and time, she sees herself as a brilliant creator with zero marketing sense.

Now that she is an adult, Janice could look objectively at her conditioning and bravely learn to cultivate her technical skills, thereby becoming a well-rounded thinker. Instead, she avoids these activities, not only because experience has convinced her that she is bad at them, but because she fears that developing her technical side will detract from her creativity.

Truth #5: *The Power of Abundance-Based Thinking*

Most of us have been conditioned to believe that we have a limited number of resources—and a limited amount of time and energy—at our disposal, and that we must measure them out carefully in order not to run out. We know that there are 24 hours in a day, and that if we spend 10 hours working, there will be only 14 left. Similarly, we are certain that if we have $100 and spend $40, we will have only $60 left. While these statements are true in the one-dimensional sense of loss and gain, we do not live in a one-dimensional world. Ours is a world of abundance, where what we stand to gain oftentimes far outweighs what we spend and give away.

You could perceive those ten hours spent working as an expenditure or loss of time, or as a wise investment that will liberate more time in the future. If you spend $40, it is true that you have $40 less right now. However, you could interpret spending (the losing and giving away of) that money as an investment (building and creating a foundation) that will or will likely result in a later gain.

The same principles apply to the mind. Spending the energy to develop your recessive skill set will not interfere in any way with your current creative or technical approach to life. In fact, it most likely will be your wisest investment, empowering and expanding the many ways you can and do think—at both the behavioral and molecular levels.

Still, many great musicians like Janice avoid learning music theory for fear that it will take them out of the "zone" and kill the "vibe" of their playing. Similarly, many successful business owners will not risk diminishing cash flows by changing their work strategies, no matter how one-dimensional or unbalanced they may be. While these practices help to ensure that they will not interfere with a system that has been producing good results, it also prevents the expansion and improvement of that system.

Cultivating her technical mind will not make Janice less of a creative artist. It will simply make her a creative artist with a cultivated technical mind, and a more well-rounded person with an expanded understanding of both her creativity and her intellect (and an ability to translate and communicate that creativity to other people). Integrating new practices into a thriving business could mean an initial decrease in productivity during the transition. But considering novel, creative ways to approach a corporate philosophy (as well as pursuing other interests and life-balancing), will most likely refresh the minds of the business owner and the staff, encourage more creative, out-of-the-box thinking, and result in a greater amount of work getting done more efficiently and effectively.

Still, "If it isn't broken, don't fix it," the saying goes, and most people remain stuck in the one-dimensional mindset that they know "works" for them. I have met brilliant performers who mistakenly resign themselves to the "fact" that they are terrible at music theory after exhausting themselves with creative approaches, and even more musicologists who continuously attempt to find the euphoria of the creative process by "thinking." The problem is not that performers are unable to understand theory, or that musicologists are lacking in creativity. The problem is that both are trying to use the one skill set that they are certain they do have to understand two very different manifestations of the one entity we call music, rather than consider that an entirely different skill set may be required for an entirely different experience of music. Thus, the either/or mentality thrives.

A Look at the Creative Mind

> ...the state of consciousness people achieve when they are so engaged in activity that nothing else seems to matter. The experience in and of itself is so rare and so enjoyable that people will seek to replicate it at great cost...[8]
>
> —Joseph Jaworski

Regardless of your conditioning or experience, I guarantee you two things. First, accessing your creative mind is imperative for optimal singing. Second, you are already a master at doing it, even if you have never considered yourself a creative person. You may not be aware when you are operating in the intuitive mode or be able to consciously access it on command yet, but you are invariably skilled in its use.

Returning to an example from a previous chapter, ask the average person to explain the process of walking. I would bet that after a concerted effort and a few frustrated attempts at an explanation, most people would not be able to come up with an acceptable answer. Too many intricate physical and mental functions and reactions occur unconsciously when walking to put them into language succinctly, if at all. Try this experiment with tying a shoe, running, sitting, standing, and talking, and you will find the same to be true.

How can this be? How can we possess information that we do not technically understand? For the same reason we discussed moments ago in the conditioning section. As children, we experienced and processed the world in a languageless, timeless, and sensory way. We observed, emotionalized, and internalized information before we ever spoke a word, and yet that information remains just as concrete and real as any mathematical formula we might be able to quantify or facts we may be able to regurgitate.

Truth #6: *Wisdom Is Everywhere*

While we cannot explain, or perhaps even logically comprehend, certain things or how we engage in certain behaviors, that does not mean that we are not fully knowledgeable. In a realm other than that of the dominant technical mind, which quickly dismisses information not packaged in a conscious, language-based format, we still "know" exactly what to do. Therefore, to truly understand wisdom, we must restate our definition to include all forms of knowledge and intelligence, both intuitive and technical.

What does being in the creative mind look and feel like now that we are adults? While each person's experience is different, some general traits have been relatively consistent in my experience with singers:

- The inner voice that you recognize as yours (the language-based chatterbox) ceases to exist and time generally becomes irrelevant—either seeming to fly by or stand still.
- Daydreams occur more frequently, usually consisting of creative realizations or intuitive understandings that exist out of real-time.
- Emotions are generally very intense, yet peaceful, soothing, and calm in nature.
- Things that once seemed like challenges seem effortless. The process of trying to understand new concepts becomes fun and pleasurable.

- Frustrations and worries seem to dissipate, and solutions to even complex problems seem obvious and uncomplicated. (Imagine a tightly bound knot releasing and untying itself in slow motion, as if underwater.)
- The feeling of being a dispassionate observer rather than a controlling participator takes over.
- Visions become more regular and profound, along with the ability to see (not define with language) solutions to long-term problems.
- Hunches, rather than logic, lead to completely effective, dependable, and predictable actions and outcomes.

For me, the creative experience is similar to what athletes and others call "being in the zone"—a place of languageless flow and boundless creativity. In this place, time seems to stop, the critical aspect of the ego disappears, and understanding floods in from all angles. Wonder abounds, and miracles seem to happen while frustration with the learning process dissipates. A client once described the feeling as "floating on a subtle tightrope wire, where every slip is a graceful fall revealing a strength and an opportunity to do better the next time." Powerful stuff, certainly more so than frustrated, judgment-based attempts to sing perfectly!

Fran Tarkenton, former quarterback of the Minnesota Vikings, recounts a story of two teammates that beautifully depicts the sensations of the creative experience:

> He would "see" the ball in the hands of the receiver before the play would ever run. He would look at his receiver and call the play, and the two of them would see the play as being completed. As he would begin to run the play, he would have a kind of clarity that he said was hard to describe. He and the receiver were in complete accord. Things would slow down and be almost effortless. He knew even before the ball ever left his hands that it was a completed pass.[9]

We find another great example in Bill Russell's book, *Second Wind*:

> Every so often a Celtic game would heat up so that it became more than a physical or even a mental game, and would be magical. That feeling is very difficult to describe, and I certainly never talked about it when I was playing. When it happened, I could feel my play rise to a new level. It came rarely, and would last anywhere from five minutes to a whole quarter or more… At that special level, all sorts of odd things happened. The game would be in a white heat of competition, and yet somehow I would not feel competitive… I would be putting out the maximum effort… and yet I never felt the pain. The game would move so quickly that every fake, cut and pass would be surprising, and yet nothing could surprise me. It was almost as if we were playing in slow motion.[10]

The Science of the Zone

> When meditating or engaged in focused concentration, the brain creates strong electromagnetic signals of around 7 to 9 Hertz (Hz) also called Alpha waves. When athletes are in "the Zone"—that place where athletic performance almost magically excels—certain patterns of increased Alpha waves typically precede, and even appear to enable, such moments of peak performance.[11]
>
> —Bryan Reeves

Continuing research is lending physiologically testable credibility to what one might otherwise attribute to personal perception. UCLA professor and researcher Dr. Valerie Hunt has dedicated her life to establishing the correlation between these "zone" experiences and neuro- and biochemical makeup. In her book, *Infinite Mind*, she cites the example of professional dancer Emilie Conrad:

> Minutes into a dance routine, electrical activity in the musculature diminished while brain or "Mind Field" activity began to skyrocket. What Emilie explained as "creating a field of energy and riding it" proved to be more than a function of perception… the mind was—and is—able to create and pattern electromagnetic energy fields which can in turn shape the physical structure of our bodies.[12]

In his research, Reeves cites biomedical engineer Itzhak Bentov's discovery of how a natural 7 Hz Alpha-like signal works rhythmically inside of the body during meditative and zone experiences, connecting the skeleton and inner organs with the heart in a resonant dance that enables the heart to work less in driving the body. Reeves goes on to note: "Interestingly, the Earth's natural electromagnetic field frequencies are measured daily to average around 7.8 Hz (called the Shumann Resonance) by scientists at UC-Berkeley's Seismology Laboratory. This natural average frequency at the earth's surface is similar to the 7 to 9 Hz Alpha frequencies emitted by the human brain in states of mediation, calm, and exceptional performance; the brain's relaxation signal is identical to the earth's natural frequency!"

What do this and other new research mean for us as singers? The body, when engaged in the zone of singing (or any activity) is closer to a state of meditation than stress, closer to a natural process than a forced one. The mind and body are in many ways working less, not more.

Accessing the Creative Mind

While these peak and zone experiences have always resonated with my experience of singing, accessing my creative mind does not always come to me automatically, especially when music is missing from the equation. Since childhood, I had considered myself to be a bad visual artist, as nothing I had ever tried to draw or paint looked like art to me. As time passed, this conviction meant that a beautiful product could never emerge from my attempts, no matter how much natural talent I might have had. (Here, once again, was neuro-linguistic programming in a less-than-shining moment.)

Thankfully, in my junior year of college I had a pivotal experience that changed everything. The class (a music class, interestingly) was my first experience with Betty Edwards' book, *Drawing on the Right Side of the Brain*,[13] our textbook for the semester. Betty, referring to the popular "right and left brain" model, uses methods to trick the dominant, technical brain out of its stubborn and critical belief systems long enough to allow the mind to try different—and usually better—approaches to creating art. The results were marvelous: not only did I enjoy the process immensely, I framed some of the pieces I created, completely dumbfounded that they came from my hand.

It is not that I could not draw; I had just never given myself the chance to see correctly and to document those visions correctly. Even though I have strong creative tendencies, my self-judgment and insecurities about my ability with visual art, coupled with my well-practiced technical tools, prevented me from operating in the creative realm. Similarly, many exceptionally creative visual artists revert to the technical when asked to sing a simple melody. Doubts and fears step in, and they overthink themselves into ineffective inaction.

Fortunately, the exercises in the book caused a shift in my fundamental thinking long enough for me to simply enjoy the creative process without qualification. Once I stopped judging myself, I was able to draw and paint some rather beautiful things.

Truth #7: *Making the Shift*

We can't expect to be able to resolve any complex problems within the same state of consciousness that created them.

—Albert Einstein

In order to succeed in accessing your creative mind, you cannot use the tools of the technical. You have to let go and have faith in your ability to access a different way of thinking. With the technical mind convinced that it can handle any- and everything that comes its way, however, it is not enough simply to expect it to make a graceful exit just because the internal creator is better equipped to handle a given situation. We rarely hear from the creative mind unless we can somehow distract the technical. This does not happen voluntarily in most people, so you must consciously and carefully construct a plan of action.

According to Betty Edwards, the only way to ensure the technical mind's exit is to coerce it into believing that the task at hand is far too insignificant to be worthy of its esteemed attention. With no awards to win, no important information to qualify, and no risk of ego jeopardy, the technical inhibitors will usually turn their focus away from the "petty" activity, thus leaving the creative mind to take over.

Going back to an example from the aforementioned music class my junior year, my technical brain could think of nothing more insignificant than an assignment that would require spending hours copying an unrecognizable object freehand. It tried in the beginning, but with nothing new to create, no time frame within which to work, and no grade to receive, it got bored and left—thinking the task far too unimportant and inconsequential. When all potential technical stimuli were blocked, the creative mind was allowed to emerge.

It turns out that the "unrecognizable image" was in fact Pablo Picasso's "Portrait of Igor Stravinsky," only turned upside down! Had the image been right side up, you can bet that my technical mind would not have dreamed of passing up an opportunity to manhandle an imitation of a work by a great master. Fortunately, it did not have the chance. By the time the exercise was finished, the technical mind had no choice but to stand back and marvel at the creative mind's seemingly newfound ability to draw.

The Creative Mind in Singing

In singing, the same holds true: it is inhibition that impedes the existing creative mind, not an inherent lack of creative vision or ability.[14] You may have difficulty singing, but that does not mean that you do not inherently have the tools to do so effortlessly. You are likely just unaware of them because you have been approaching the information incorrectly.

Consider the Irish people and African-American churchgoers we discussed in chapter two. Overall, they are not more creative or intuitive or talented than the rest of us.[15] Rather, their societies do not require the inhibition of singing. Similarly, Aida's family found a way to prevent the cultural inhibition of her natural singing process. It remained an integrated and automatic response, not succumbing to a compressed technical understanding or the attachment of self-consciousness.

When all potential technical stimuli were blocked, the creative mind was allowed to emerge.

When someone says, "Take a deep breath, engage your diaphragm, and lift your palate," they are speaking the language of the factual inhibitor and inviting it in. Similarly, if a "Forget what you know; you must learn this way" approach is also in the mix—especially if feelings of inadequacy or guilt are involved or encouraged—then you have the societal, emotional inhibitor in play as well. Both factors will ensure a non-integrated methodology of voice production; thus, the prevalence of drug and alcohol use in performers seeking to combat these common forms of inhibition.

Factual explanations do not work, nor, in the long term, do drugs and alcohol. Observation, imitation, and trial-and-error do.[16] This is the science behind the effectiveness of sensory, intuitive, non-verbal learning. That is what Myra taught me all those years ago, and what I try to share with my clients. By accessing the original method of natural sound production, the inhibitors are bypassed and information is not only taken in, but internalized deep in our emotional centers and wholly retained. The process, like walking and talking, becomes automated and automatic, as well as effortless.

To do this, you must initially create an environment that is consistently free of:
- Time limits
- Judgment
- Language-based explanations
- Qualification
- Ego-involvement
- Pressure
- Fear
- Emotional danger

This is an amazing challenge, given that most of us have been conditioned to believe that to do anything well requires constant observation, self-critique, and analysis—particularly in the case of singing. While this holds true for many technical activities, again, the creative mind functions in a completely different way.

You will not paint a more beautiful picture if you are constantly looking at your watch, trying to ascertain how masterful your half-painted picture looks. Similarly, you will not sing with more emotion and power if you are stopping every minute to decide whether you sound like Maria Callas or Frank Sinatra. Still, I recall almost identical first experiences with virtually all of my clients: the watching, judging, controlling, listening, and critiquing begin almost before the first note is even thought of!

The body therefore never fully relaxes, and unnecessary musculature is always engaged and ready to further constrict at the first sign of a potentially imperfect tone.

Although letting go of control may be completely contrary to your nature, it is the first step in improving your singing. Remember, the creative mind is always engaged and functioning in its natural process, though it is sometimes covered over by the technical mind's loud and often fearful attempts to control, manhandle, and inhibit the process. But once the voice is released and the shift made back into the creative mind (as in the process of speaking), intuition, observation, and flow again take over. Tensions dissipate and the natural voice returns. From there, careful practice (physical and mental) and retraining of the muscle memory will help recreate the consistency of that freedom, thus allowing you to return there again and again.

Imagine that you have been given a kite. If you are determined to help it fly by holding it tight, it will remain lifeless in your grip. However, if you trust the connection of the string to the kite, realizing that in the seemingly tenuous relationship lies the potential for all guidance, the kite will soar and sail. By holding just the string, you are able to make large adjustments to the kite's flight path with small, gentle movements of your fingers. You have gained control by letting go. With singing, it is the same.

In his book *Synchronicity*, author Joseph Jaworski describes a skeet shooting experience with an important lesson. He was in the zone and doing beautifully, not missing any of the targets, until someone told him that he needed only one more to get a perfect score. "At that point, I started trying, and I missed."[17]

Until you become adept at staying in the creative mind, you will have tough moments, moments when you fall out of the zone. When the ego decides to get re-involved and inhibit the natural process, we find ourselves snapped suddenly out of the feeling of oneness we had been experiencing with our activity; the kite falls from the sky and gets crumpled in our hands. Remember, though, that returning to your best voice is only—and literally—a few thoughts away.

When and How We Need the Technical Mind

We have spent an awful lot of time criticizing the inhibitors, detailing the many ways they can interfere with creativity and the healthy singing process. It may therefore seem like the last thing we want is to explore how to bring them back in. But once an on-command, second-nature vocal connection is reestablished and harmful technical habits eradicated, the one-time bad guys can become our greatest allies.

The Technical Mind as Protector

Just as many creative people need someone to help them with the business and scheduling of their day-to-day lives, the technical mind in its correct function serves as the creative mind's caretaker. With its arsenal of facts, rules, and regulations, it is now in the perfect position to manage the intuitive mind out in the world. The technician says, "You create, and I'll make sure everyone sees your beautiful creations." What a relationship!

With such close proximity, what keeps the technical mind from jumping right back into inhibiting the natural process of singing? Remember, once we have reconnected to the intuitive experience and made it a habit, the technical mind no longer feels the need to inhibit the activity. Once it realizes (that is, once it has been tricked into realizing) that the creator is the better singer, it will find new roles. The challenge is to help it find and excel in those of equally great importance: monitoring, analyzing, and protecting.

Let us refer again to the experience of walking. When you walk, you are not conscious of the myriad brain signals and muscular movements involved with each step. The unconscious mind is blissfully handling all that, because the technical mind decided long ago that walking is a boring process, with no ego validation. However, when a big pothole appears in the middle of the road, the technical mind jumps onto the scene as the hero once again. "Look out," it says. "We don't want to trip and fall and look like a total clod!" It has been totally helpful, and while it may linger around for a while to make sure that things are safe, it will promptly return from walking monitor back to whatever very important task it was concerning itself with before the crisis.

The technical mind in its correct function serves as the creative mind's caretaker.

Coping With Real-Life Problems That Affect the Voice

It is the same in singing. While distraction leads many artists to snap out of their creative zones, the technical mind can prevent disaster by handling any pitfalls or roadblocks, both preemptively and in the moment that could cause a glitch in the creative mind's immersion in activity. Beyond external distractions, the technical mind is also enormously helpful in dealing with more specifically singing-related challenges:

- Illness
- Allergy
- Crisis (perceived or real)
- Nervousness (stage fright)
- New material in unfamiliar ranges
- Songs in new languages
- Studio recording
- Live performance

Remember that both the creative and technical minds have their roles. The creative is the singer and the technical is the monitor. So, what would happen if only the creative mind were engaged in a time of crisis? Nothing short of trouble: either an oblivious singer fearlessly powering through potentially damaging circumstances or a disconnection from creative activity (its real job), causing a diminished performance as well as stress and panic.

Even if you have never had a serious vocal crisis resulting in surgery or prolonged vocal rest, you most likely have felt performance jitters before a show, stress at the time of a recording session, or the dread of managing a cold during an important rehearsal. With the creative mind still responsible for a great performance, it is now the technician's role to monitor and manage the situation's new variables, keeping them out of the hands of the singer. Whether you are nervous, congested, or in an unfamiliar environment, you will be creating sound in the same physical manner, though you may need an extra boost of support or a slight variance in placement to ensure the best tone. With the technical mind taking note of new variables and communicating what last-minute modifications to mindset and technique might be needed, a favorable performance is achieved.

Mastering the Space

I was recently helping a client prepare to record her new album. We had been working together in my studio for approximately two months and the songs were coming together beautifully. She is a successful recording artist with a very healthy self-confidence and sense of her voice, so making minor vocal and artistic modifications was an effortless experience for both of us.

On her first day of recording, we met at the recording studio to warm up in the new vocal booth where she would be singing. The problems began instantly. In each song, she had a great deal of trouble freeing her always-open voice. She tried to use her throat, rather than air, to create expression, a practice unheard of in our time together.

On a hunch, I had her leave the vocal booth (approximately 7 x 7 feet, with dark, padded walls and no windows) and enter the open recording room (which, at approximately 25 x 35 feet, was a much airier, lighter space… similar to my studio). I asked her to start the song we had just been going through. After one line, her eyes shot open and her jaw dropped in shock. The tight and tense voice that she had been struggling to relax over the past 15 minutes opened right up and filled the room.

I say "filled the room" because that is exactly what happened, from the mind's eye of her intuitive self. In a small, cramped, and virtually soundproof space, her creative mind unconsciously adapted by struggling to create the same emotional and vocal ring that she was used to hearing elsewhere. This is a virtually impossible task in a room designed to absorb sound.

The dance between the intuitive mind and the technical mind in their correct roles begins, resulting in beautiful, healthy singing.

Her creative mind was completely unaware of these adjustments, though her throat and ears knew something was wrong. In all her years of recording (usually in an open space), her experience of singing was so natural, so second-nature, that she was unable to understand and process the impact of the space and its relevance to her performance. This inability was further exacerbated by her neglect of the development of her technical mind, similar to Janice, over the years.

She ultimately recorded the whole album in the larger space, which resulted in another beautiful, powerful, and successful recording. Afterward, we focused on sensitizing her technical filters to recognize and handle the adjustments in space perception necessary to enable her, under any circumstances, to sing naturally.

The technical mind is just as crucial in live singing. Whether you are using in-ear or onstage monitors, the monitor mix, the room size and structure, and the acoustics all affect the performance experience, making each unique not only from one another, but from the natural singing experience. Left alone, a singer will unconsciously try to adjust the voice to overcompensate for these differences—particularly in the case of monitors that fit directly in the ear cavity (in-ear monitors). But with the help of cold cognition, the singer can go on doing what he or she does best, while the technical mind lends a hand to assess what audio variables have come into play and translate this information in a way that allows the singer to engage the voice naturally without compensation.[18]

Whether new audio variables, space perception, illness, or fear, it is the role of the technical mind to take a hard look at the origin of these stressors and to work to manage them on behalf of the singer and the performance. With this dynamic in place, the dance between the intuitive mind and the technical mind in their correct roles begins, resulting in beautiful, healthy singing.

Chapter 6

Fear and the Psychology of Singing

There are costs and risks to a program of action, but they are far less than the long-range risks and costs of comfortable inaction.

—John F. Kennedy

When working with new clients, I always begin by trying to ascertain what it is about their voices that they perceive as problematic or would like to improve. Their desires run the gamut from increased power, range, and pitch accuracy to cultivating a more relaxed and natural tone. Although the factors that prevent them from achieving these goals may, on the surface, seem entirely related to the voice (throat tension and discomfort; inadequate, poor, or disconnected breath support; unattractive tone), I estimate that over 90% of vocal troubles are caused and/or exacerbated by some form of fear, insecurity, or lack of self-confidence.

Can fear really cause so many problems? Absolutely. Even if you have decided how you want to experience your voice, redefined your relationship to singing, changed your language patterns, implemented positive NLP, and learned how to approach singing in a way that best suits your learning and thinking preferences, your voice will never be clear and healthy as long as you have unmanaged fears standing in your way.

Your voice will never be clear and healthy as long as you have unmanaged fears standing in your way.

Unfortunately, it is hard to deal with the fears in our lives when most of us turn and run when we are faced with situations that make us feel scared, intimidated, or out of control. Even though fears affect everyone (especially performers) at every stage of life, the fact that it is generally socially unacceptable to talk about them makes matters worse, helping to ensure that most of us become experts at avoiding, ignoring, or overcompensating for them.

Sometimes fear is conscious, but very often we repress it entirely… Unspoken fears create blocks or crimps in the body's energy flow, and it is these blocks that ultimately result in problems. The fears keep manifesting in ever-greater degrees until we deal with them. Physical problems are the last step. Ideally these blocks would be dealt with early, in a preventative way, before illness develops.[1]

—James Redfield

Even if you have developed a good system for getting your fears out of the way, they never really go very far. Just as our bodies are quick to tell us when we need more sleep, more exercise, a better diet, or less stress, we get physical reminders of all the fear, anger, and sadness that we do not fully process and release. Before we know it, they manifest as tension, pain, and even disease, wreaking havoc on our health, optimism, and voices.

Instead of taking the hint, most of us get irritated when our bodies do not act perfectly. We pop aspirin for headaches, antacids for heartburn, and pills for back pain rather than consider that perhaps our bodies are trying to tell us something—for our own benefit. We dull the physical symptoms rather than deal with the realities of our feelings, relationships, and lives.

Where Do Our Fears Come From?

While we can accumulate fears at any point, in my experience the majority are developed in childhood and brought consciously and unconsciously into adulthood for two reasons:

- We believe that our fears are valid.
- We feel unable to make them go away.

There are various drama-producing situations we may have encountered in childhood that can cause us to experience feelings of inadequacy and fear, including:

- Being harshly judged
- Being overly criticized
- Not receiving approval
- Not feeling respected
- Not feeling or receiving love
- Being ignored
- Being mistreated
- Being abused verbally or physically
- Not being validated for who we are or what we do

While being ignored or not receiving approval may not conjure up feelings of fear in you today (anger or a compulsive desire to impress are much more typical adult reactions), they most likely did when you were a child. Children tend to take responsibility not only for their feelings, but also for the feelings and actions of those around them, internalizing everything short of unconditional love and approval as "Something is inherently wrong with me." No matter how abusive, moody, unhappy, fearful, angry, or neglectful parents are, children tend to perceive that some terrible action or inherent unworthiness of their own must have caused the unrest in the home.

Just because you do not consciously feel emotions relating to your childhood does not mean they do not exist. The fears you felt when you were five are still present in your life if you did not have a healthy outlet for them back then and have yet to take a critical look at how they have manifested in your life today. It seems silly for a 30-year-old to be afraid of the dark and unknown, though, so your brilliant mind renames the manifestation of your childhood fear "insomnia," your fear of abandonment "co-dependency," your sibling rivalry "competitiveness," your fear of not being good enough "perfectionism," and your desire for more love and attention "neediness" and "insecurity." Thus, our fears remain with us as we transition to adulthood.

Fortunately, we now have the wherewithal to realize that the actions of our parents and others in our lives were primarily the result of their own issues, rather than a reflection of any inadequacy on our part. Most people never really learn this, though, because it requires having to work through the pain and fear that we have all spent a lifetime trying to repress.

What Fear Can Do: Manifestations in Singing

What do these conscious and unconscious fears have to do with singing? Everything! Fear, by its very nature, is a call for self-protection and inhibition. As such, it ensures that the transition to the intuitive mode never fully occurs. The ability to be open, vulnerable, and brave; to take chances, explore, and play… fear prevents us from fully experiencing these things. Great singing requires a confidence that unmanaged fears will never allow, and no amount of technique—no matter how sound and solid—will be beneficial in combating tensions that exist *because* of fear and insecurity. Therefore, an integrated approach, one that addresses both the voice and the mind, is required for optimal vocal development.

Fortunately, we now have the wherewithal to realize that the actions of our parents and others in our lives were primarily the result of their own issues, rather than a reflection of any inadequacy on our part.

Shame

Julianna came to me wanting to learn how to relax her throat and let her voice go. She is not a professional singer, nor does she want to be. She simply wanted to learn how to get back to the place she knew in childhood where singing was effortless and fun.

Julianna is a large woman with an enormous presence and an even larger voice… until she starts to sing. Like Barbara from chapter two, Julianna's loud and brilliant laugh and voice turned quiet and mouse-like as she began to sing through a spiritual that she had brought to our first session. Her relaxed physical energy became rigid and closed off as she worked her way through the song, guarding and controlling each note with a clenched throat. A variety of relaxation techniques and centering breathing exercises, while helpful, could not diminish her persistence in singing with a cautious tone through rigid musculature.

Upon closer observation, the cause of her voice troubles became clear. "Ladies," her family and teachers said, "were meant to be quiet and reserved, not big and brash." It turns out the criticism was being aimed at her weight, but expanded in Julianna's mind to include all aspects of being "big." She therefore spent her childhood feeling ashamed of her outgoing personality and rich voice, which served to squash both her vocal and personal joy.

Once she learned to address and release the hold her community and family opinions still had on her, she was able to create new relationships with her voice and her body. By letting go of the judgment and shame she felt toward herself—mind, body, and spirit—for being big, outgoing, and filled with energy, she was able to explore both the gloriously huge voice and personality that had been waiting for years to emerge.

Anger

Patricia came to me as a frustrated singer/songwriter wanting to trade in her "pretty" and "trained" sound for one with rawer texture and edge. She desperately wanted to let go and express the emotion and passion that she felt inside, but could not seem to overcome all the classical training she had received.

It was somewhat clear to Patricia that her vocal dilemma mirrored that of her own life.

As in Julianna's case, issues from the past played an enormous role in Patricia's troubles. Despite her claims of wanting to let go, Patricia carried a tremendous amount of tension in both her body and voice, and for very good reason. As a child, she was locked in a closet and punished severely for emotional outbursts, particularly outbursts of anger. To make matters worse, she was required to maintain a loving façade throughout her teen years, pretending to be content and happy around the very people who had caused her so much pain. With nowhere else to go, the anger manifested itself as physical ailment after physical ailment throughout her life, including her current plights of chronic fatigue syndrome and fibromyalgia.

It was somewhat clear to Patricia that her vocal dilemma mirrored that of her own life, an awareness that made it easier for us to deal with and work through. The feelings of anger and agony from her childhood were still too raw to address directly, though, so we used the vehicle of singing to combat these issues. After creating a space where she felt safe to experiment with me and with her voice, we were able to work with some emotional yelling and yelping exercises to let go of the repressed anger and rage that had lived inside her for decades. This served not only to release these pent-up feelings, but her voice as well, by using the vehicle of the open, loud, and out-of-control sounds that Patricia had hitherto felt were inappropriate or not permitted. Once she was able to express and overcome the guilt she felt for her anger, her vocal tensions subsided and her voice came to an emotional and performative center in which she felt safe and comfortable.

Control

Peter came to me longing to "get out of his own way." His mind and his voice seemed to want two completely different things and were constantly in battle. He had a lovely tone and a great sense of pitch, but would persistently tighten, strain, and overwork his instrument. Even when his voice escaped, sounding free and extraordinary, in a matter of moments he would return to clenching his chest, throat, and neck, convinced that his voice was "going all over the place" and "becoming out of control."

Peter was able to recognize the relationship between his desire to maintain control and his fears of failure and rejection.

After secretly recording a few of our sessions together, I was able to demonstrate to Peter that he was not hearing his voice correctly. What he thought was a bad sound was really a feeling he was uncomfortable with: freedom. He was baffled to discover the disparity between what he had perceived to be good singing and the tight and rigid sounds he was actually making when he tried to remain in control. Still, he continued to panic and repeatedly returned to tightening and straining his instrument in spite of the realization that releasing the voice was correct and that, with the affirmation of the tape, it sounded great.

His singing-related fears paralleled those in his life: so long as he maintained rigid control of himself and every situation in which he found himself, he would not have to deal with the fear of spinning out of control. He had a decision to make. He could either continue to try to control outcomes, or relax and let go: to sound tense or sound great.

After some conscious attention, Peter was able to recognize the relationship between his desire to maintain control and his fears of failure and rejection. He also realized that his dislike of his voice really had nothing to do with his voice; it was really a dislike of aspects of himself that caused him to feel his voice was inadequate. Once he started working through these issues, the grip of control started to ease, along with the tension in his voice. Today he is able to approach singing with openness and wonder, eager to try new things and have new experiences.

Ego

Fear of Success/Fear of Failure

Feelings of sadness, anxiety, and depression are common emotions that plague those unsure of their inherent worthiness. While some find the courage to deal with these feelings of inadequacy head-on, others seek salvation in an external force that they perceive will "save them" by making them feel valid.

In my experience, this is the one of the most prevalent issues in professional performance. So many people I work with look to their music careers with an obsessed uneasiness, desperate to become famous and/or rich, two of the more common validation goals that I have seen.

They have conscious thoughts that stand in for, or reveal, underlying unconscious ones:

Conscious thought	Unconscious thought
If I am famous, then I'll be happy.	I am unhappy now and incapable of making myself happy without outside validation.
I'll be loved by everyone.	I don't feel loved or loveable now.
People will think that I am talented and important.	I fear that I have no inherent talent. I feel that my opinion doesn't count and that I am not important.
If I am rich, then I'll be happy.	I am afraid that I am not powerful enough to create, engage in, or maintain a successful and lucrative business.
I won't have to worry about how I'll make a living.	I am terrified of being poor and unable to support myself.
I can spend my time doing whatever I want.	I don't believe that I am powerful enough to make a living doing what I want.

Unfortunately, these aspirations, along with the hoped-for outcomes, are seriously flawed. To begin, most people forget that being rich and famous requires being in the public eye where they will be seen, scrutinized, and criticized. That is not going to sit so well if they feel unconsciously certain of their inherent unworthiness and are terrified of everyone else coming to the same conclusion.

If we are not centered and confident in ourselves, the strains of life in the public eye can be overwhelmingly debilitating and unbearable.

If we are not centered and confident in ourselves, the strains of life in the public eye can be overwhelmingly debilitating and unbearable. Most people do not see this when they are setting their sights on the prize, though. All the fearful child inside sees is a potential way out of feeling worthless. But as success looms near, most people figure out pretty quickly that this idea probably was not such a good one, and then all hell breaks loose at one of two points along the way.

Problems Arising Prior to Achieving Success

If you desperately want to achieve a goal, but are terrified that you will fail at it, what would be the easiest way to avoid dealing with success and/or failure? This may seem like a trick question, but I watch client after client find the answer to this sad riddle by developing problems with their voices.

With patience, Deborah recognized that her frenzied quest for fame was, in many ways, an effort to escape from feeling inadequate, unworthy, abandoned, and terrified that she would never amount to anything.

Deborah was on her way to a career as recording artist, with a tremendous live show and a respectable following. She had some tensions in her voice that we were actively working on, but nothing that would interfere with a healthy performance career. Then a stroke of "bad luck" hit.

About the same time the record labels were starting to take a serious interest in Deborah, she developed an uncommon condition called spasmodic vocal dysphonia, a neurological disorder characterized by perpetual muscle spasms in the throat that cause the voice to warble uncontrollably. Imagine her devastation and frustration. Here she was, on the brink of achieving the dreams she had worked toward throughout her life, and now those dreams were about to go down the tubes.

My suggestion that she consider the possibility of a mental component to the problem was met with shock, disbelief, and anger. She denied feeling any fear of singing or of signing a record deal. For goodness' sake, this was what she wanted! Only after becoming extremely desperate did she consider my suggestion to look critically at the potential fears and emotions she may have been harboring.

With time, Deborah was able to see that she had been running so fast for so long toward her dream that she had never really taken the time to confront the non-music-related insecurities in her life. With patience, she recognized that her frenzied quest for fame was, in many ways, an effort to escape from feeling inadequate, unworthy, abandoned, and terrified that she would never amount to anything. Now that she was close to achieving the validation she so desperately longed for, she was faced with some staggering questions: What happens if the one thing I have thought will make me feel valid does not do the trick? What happens if I am rejected or if people don't like me? Only when she recognized that she would always be worthy, regardless of what happened in her career, was she able to healthily redefine and follow her dreams.

Not everyone is struck suddenly with such a severe ailment (and, of course, not all ailments are necessarily related to a mental component), but that does not mean that minor problems do not stem from the same types of issues. Sore throats, aches, allergies, excessive mucus drainage, illnesses, muscle cramps, and other physical symptoms seem to arise like clockwork when we are on the verge of important career events and performances. Why? Because it is scarier to pursue your life dream completely healthy and prepared than to have an excuse for why you did not achieve your goals, in the event that things do not go the way you want them to.

When we crack during a song, do not get a gig we are auditioning for, or in general do not like the way we sound, it softens the blow to have something or someone else to blame. And what better to blame your shortcomings on? Our bodies are the perfect targets. They are not going to speak up like a friend or family member and say, "Hey wait a minute! You can't blame this on me!"

Auditions and performances can be nerve-wracking, for sure. But having an excuse ("I'm sick." "I'm not warmed up." "I'm so tired.") generally translates to a more distracted and less authentic and moving performance. Do not do this to yourself! Go into all auditions and performances with the idea that you will give your 100% and shine. So what if you are not feeling well? Unless you choose to turn around and go home, there is nothing you can do about it. The situation is out of your control. Therefore, commit to always doing your very, very best. No matter your health or emotions, your body, mind, and voice will conspire to function at a much higher level if you are wholly committed than if you are over thinking and stressed out.

It takes a lot of confidence to accept responsibility for all our actions—in every area of our lives—knowing that sometimes our best might not be what someone else is looking for. Realizing that other people's lack of approval isn't necessarily indicative of shortcomings on our part is an important key to fully pursuing our dreams and enjoying the process.

Realizing that other people's lack of approval isn't necessarily indicative of shortcomings on our part is an important key to fully pursuing our dreams and enjoying the process.

Problems Arising After Success Is Achieved

On the other side of the coin, I have many clients who sailed straight through the "becoming famous" stage, only to develop a host of mysterious illnesses once they achieved the spotlight they had so desperately longed for. Confused and frightened, it is then that they call me, looking for help.

Mike and Eric are both phenomenal singers with successful careers as recording artists. Both have millions of adoring fans, both have released a number of hit records that gained critical acclaim, and now, both of them cannot sing.

It may seem unfathomable, but think honestly about how the body is the easiest place to lay blame in their situations. It would be terrible to say, "Now that I am in a position that most people would die to be in, I am going to give up because I am terrified and miserable," especially when they (and a team of people) have devoted so much time and energy to their success. Again, the body becomes the easy target: "I would love to do another record. I would give anything to go on tour, but every time I open my mouth to sing, I just can't! I know the doctors say there is nothing wrong with my throat, but I'm telling you that I can't sing. Listen to how bad I sound!"

And they do sound bad. Their throats are tight and tense. Their tones are pinched and their breath support is completely off-kilter. They are unable to sustain notes, unable to remain on pitch, and unable to sing for long periods of time without becoming hoarse and fatigued. These physical problems are not figments of their imaginations; they are real, even though their cause is mental. The decision to compromise their vocal health in order to avoid dealing with their fears is not a conscious one; they are desperate for solutions when they come to me.

As long as a person's sense of self revolves around an external factor, whether it is career, money, or another person's presence, approval, or validation, it is impossible to be truly happy and content. When we do not find happiness in the external place where we have decided happiness lives, it is easy to understand why our worlds feel like they are crumbling. I do not have enough fingers and toes to count the stories of successful artists who fall apart, even though they seem to have everything a person could want. Whether it is drugs, alcohol, illness, fanaticism, or even death, so many artists find escape routes from the lives of wealth and public attention they were once convinced would make them happy.

The trouble with these escape routes is that they are usually circular in design, eventually leading us right back to where we started: back into our feelings of inadequacy. While it may feel like you are afraid of being a singer, your fear most likely has nothing to do with singing. Singing is simply the place you find your sense of adequacy and self, and therefore, where your mind decides to manifest your fears (of failure, of success, of abandonment, etc.), in the hopes that you will pay attention. Leave the music business, though, and what seemed like career- and music-related stress will continue to reappear in other forms and in other places until you pay attention.

Singers are not the only ones who find themselves confronted with achievement trauma. While many athletes might not care about whether or not they can sing, they care about stress strains and fractures. Violinists care about their hands trembling, and business owners care about high blood pressure and heart attacks. Changing jobs, taking a vacation, or seeing a massage therapist may temporarily alleviate some of the tensions, fears, and frustrations that seem to come from a stressful occupation, but unmanaged, they will be back.

Redefining Our Relationship to Fear

…the only thing we have to fear is fear itself.[2]

—Franklin D. Roosevelt

Roosevelt's famous line has been used repeatedly as a useful motivation tool, encouraging people to achieve their dreams by conquering their fears. But what happens to those fears? Have they really been conquered, or simply hushed and pushed farther away by a barrage of positive determination? While Roosevelt's quote may be powerful for some, in my opinion it is better framed as:

"We have nothing to fear but an unhealthy relationship to fear."

Contrary to popular belief, fear is not the enemy. An unhealthy relationship with fear is. Every message that our body sends encourages us to take a critical look at the way we are living, and to make adjustments for the better. Who else would our bodies be rooting for, anyway? Therefore, the best first step in dealing with fear is to move toward it, rather than try to make it disappear.

Truth #8: *Fear Is Wisdom*

You may be amazed to find that the fear-filled voices that have been depressing, oppressing, and nagging you for years do not get louder when you finally pay attention. Like a screaming child, they simply want to be acknowledged, and will begin to diminish when you listen to what they have to say. Once we place our fears in perspective by removing the element of panic, they become calls to action, as opposed to the familiar signal to run and hide. What once were painful and paralyzing forces are now opportunities to learn and grow. As Deborah put it:

> After tuning in to my fears of performing, I realized it wasn't performing I
> was afraid of; it was my fear of being a failure, of messing up. I was constantly
> terrified of performing for fear of making a mistake, no matter how small.
> When I looked deeper into this fear, I realized that my performance anxiety
> was really a fear of being seen, of people seeing that I wasn't worthy of

their attention. I originally thought this was silly, but when I looked more closely, I remembered that throughout my childhood, my mom was always laughing at me whenever I would mess up at anything, no matter how insignificant. Looking closer, I see that my grandparents treated my mom the same way, and that her laughter at me really wasn't about me, it was simply an ingrained reflex she had unconsciously kept with her since childhood and projected onto me.

Realizations, like this one Deborah had during a session, are powerful. They tap into the core of the fear and help it begin to dissipate through understanding. From that moment on, every time Deborah felt overwhelmingly afraid of messing up, she realized that she still had some work to do with redefining her relationship with her past. Listening to her fears and enacting a policy of honest self-assessment helped her become more centered as a person, not just as a singer. Most importantly, she followed her revelations with action by beginning to restructure her relationships to herself, her career, and her voice.

Truth #9: *The Reality of the Reward*

Patterns of any kind, no matter how engrained, dissipate when you offer yourself a better reward.

If you are terrified to sing, panicked in your desire to become famous, or certain that your talent is not that great, you cannot possibly have a healthy relationship with your voice, no matter how often you swear up and down that you want one. So why not simply quit, or adjust your thinking? Because on some level, conscious or unconscious, you are deriving a benefit from the situation you are currently in, and that benefit is greater than your true desire to change and greater than your perception of the benefit of the new situation.

This is an incredibly important concept, so let me say it again: You are deriving some benefit from any and every situation you are currently in, and that benefit is greater than your true desire to change.

Not only can we calm our fear, but we can also alter a vast majority of our circumstances with nothing more than the decision to embrace our fears and apply their wisdom. Not so, say most people. "I didn't choose to have such a crappy job. I didn't choose to be broke. I didn't choose to have a bad marriage or ungrateful children." Ah, but most likely—on some level—you did.

To discuss the concepts of taking responsibility and creating outcomes properly and fully would require a separate book, and fortunately, there are many great ones written on the subject. For our purposes, let's explore this issue by looking at one of the examples from above: a bad marriage. (Feel free to pick a situation in your life that you truly feel is something you have not chosen for yourself.) You were young, you say. You did not know him well enough. You have changed; she has changed. You have kids now; it would be unfair to leave them. You cannot afford to be single. Your family, church, or community would disapprove of you if you got a divorce…

These things may all be true, *and* the fact remains that you not only chose that situation, for a variety of conscious and unconscious reasons, but you have chosen to remain in that situation. And, like it or not, that brings us back to the original point: you are deriving some benefit from that arrangement (proximity to your children, financial security, community approval) and that benefit is greater than the pain, frustration, and discomfort that would come from making a change, even if that change would be better in the end. In other words, you have weighed the current situation against what it would require to change the situation, and the former has won. If the opposite were true, if you perceived that the benefits of making that change outweighed the benefits of the current situation, as well as what it would take to make that change, you would indeed leave.

We cannot necessarily control everything that happens to us, but we can control our reaction to every situation.

This is true in all life situations: When your desire for a new situation and your belief in your ability to create one becomes stronger than your feelings toward your present situation and the rewards from it, you will certainly create that new reality.

Regardless of your chosen career path or personal situation, learning to believe in your ability to create authentic opportunities for yourself and enjoy the process of doing so will calm almost any fear, since your fear is most likely present as a sign that a change is advantageous and/or necessary. When you learn to have confidence in yourself and your abilities—as well as in the wisdom of your fears—you shift the power from circumstances outside of yourself into the center of your being. We cannot necessarily control everything that happens to us, but we can control our reaction to every situation. When you begin to take mental and actual action in a direction of your own choosing, you are in charge of each and every step, and, therefore, of your life.

In singing, this principle is 100% applicable. As discussed above, Mike and Eric swore up and down that they desperately wanted to heal their voices, they desperately wanted to record their new CDs, and they desperately wanted to go on tour, make money, and be there for their fans. And they did want these things, just not as much as they wanted to dwell in the comfort, however unconscious, of not having to deal with the possibilities of failure, rejection, and disapproval.

The reward system is not just about famous people making career decisions. Even though he swore that he wanted to let his voice be free, for a while Peter had decided that the reward of singing with a clenched throat (feeling in control) was greater than singing with an open one (fear of losing control). I see this weighing of options every day in my studio as singers decide how free they are actually willing to allow their voices (and themselves) to become.

Once you can accept full responsibility for the current state of your voice, your career and all of the decisions therein, performing can then again become a vehicle for expression rather than a battleground for unmanaged fear and ego. Mastering this shift can change not only your relationship to singing, but can literally change your view of the world, from one with limited resources and opportunities to an optimistic and abundant place where every goal is simply an intention, action, and reward away.

Some Tools

Listening to your fears might seem like a daunting task, especially if they always seem to be screaming at you. But remember, our fears are screaming to be heard over the incessant chatter of our minds, and will speak in a more relaxed tone when we pay attention to what they have to say. Once we develop the habit of being able to listen to our fears calmly, our panic subsides and we can get to work.

Meditation and yoga are two wonderful tools for finding the stillness that promotes centered thinking. Keeping a journal is also a great way for staying connected to your thoughts, so you can meet each fear upon its arrival, dealing with it before it has a chance to manifest physically. If journaling is not your thing or if you do not enjoy tying up your body in a pretzel, you may want to consider trying the "I feel" exercise.

Whenever you feel afraid, angry, sad, or nervous (any emotion, for that matter), stop whatever you are doing and focus completely on the emotion. Be as honest as you can and say aloud, if the situation permits: "I feel sad/angry/afraid because…" The verbalization of emotion is not only cleansing, but many times we are not totally clear on what it is we are feeling until we give those feelings direct, verbal attention. Similar to the silent exploration of emotions we've yet to process that we discussed in the language chapter, the verbal investigation of conscious emotions often provides additional insight to the extent and shape of our feelings. When you allow yourself ample space to explore your emotions consciously, you are more likely to discover the cause of each and therefore are able to prevent them from manifesting.

There is a tool frequently used with children called a "fear monster" that is wonderfully helpful for adults as well. The exercise involves finding or drawing a picture of a monster's face, and then writing upon it every single fear you feel. Symbolically, the picture of the monster (or any image you associate with fear and negativity) is powerful, but a blank piece of paper will suffice. Be thorough, take your time, and leave out no fear, no matter how simple or insignificant it may seem. When you feel satisfied that you have addressed each of your fears and that they are all before you, cut the monster's face (or piece of paper) into pieces, leaving each written fear intact.

Like anticipating the sting of an injection, the anticipation of confronting the enormity of your fears is probably greater than their reality. What once felt overwhelming and debilitating now lies before you in a visually manageable pile on a now mutilated face of what once was a monster. By categorizing your fears (separating them in piles), you may further notice that what felt like a hundred separate and powerful fears is actually a group of similar fears revolving around a few distinct themes. As most of us are largely run by unaddressed issues from our pasts, it can be a great surprise (and hopefully a great relief) to recognize that many of the fears we are still reacting to look very trivial, no longer having relevance in our adult life.[3]

Our greatest opportunities for growth and learning lie in the inevitable and unexpected challenges we encounter along our journeys.

Trivial or not, many of us have been motivated by these fears for a lifetime, and working through them will not be as simple as performing a quick self-analysis or completing a few exercises. While it took only a few paragraphs to describe the stories of Julianna, Deborah, and Peter, their journeys to resolution were in fact long and, at times, emotionally arduous.

Be patient with yourself. Joseph Campbell called the problems and fears we encounter in life "the road of trials,"[4] which in the end makes us stronger. Clearly, we can learn from our successes, but perhaps our greatest opportunities for growth and learning lie in the inevitable and unexpected challenges we encounter along our journeys.

Beneficial Fears in the Realm of Singing

Once the relationship to our fears has shifted, we are able to explore their many benefits in the realm of performing.

Stage Fright

An archer competing for a clay vessel shoots effortlessly, his skill and concentration unimpeded. If the prize is changed to a brass ornament, his hands begin to shake. If it is changed to gold, he squints as if he were going blind. His abilities do not deteriorate, but his belief in them does, as he allows the supposed value of an external reward to cloud his vision.[5]

—Chuang Tse

Shakespeare said, "All the world's a stage, and all the men and women merely players."[6] Indeed, in every interaction we are "performing." In trying to express an emotion, trying to evoke one from someone else, or even simply being, the all-familiar act of living provides us with the foundation of experience to draw upon, practice, and then portray publicly on stage. Easy, right?

Comfort with the lyrics of a song, a personal connection to the material, and knowing how you want to move onstage will surely help to curb the sensations of stage fright. Still, I have yet to meet, hear of, or work with anyone who is completely and consistently free of it, regardless of preparation, experience, psychological health, or talent.

When we step onstage to perform, our bodies are actually preparing for battle.

Is this normal? Is it possible to make the dreaded butterflies go away? Can stage fright be managed, or are we all doomed to deal with the sweating, shaking, and nerves for the duration of our careers?

While it may seem that our fear is encouraging us to run away from performance opportunities, like all fear, it is a call to action that is actually trying to prepare us for the experience. While we try desperately to relax, breathe deeply, and calm the shakes, our bodies are busy turning up the volume of our jitters. As senseless as this may seem, there is a very good reason.

Since the beginning of time, the fight-or-flight response has helped man survive in the face of an attack. In a moment of crisis, real or perceived, the brain signals for adrenaline to be released into the blood stream, causing an increase in heart rate and oxygen consumption, as well as a heightened sense of awareness—all the things needed to prepare for and cope with an attack.

While most of us no longer face the threat of being assaulted by neighboring villages or wild animals, this spontaneous response helps us deal with danger, accidents, potential aggressors, and other modern-day battles. When we are driving down a busy street and someone pulls out in front of us, we do not stop to think. Our bodies instantly kick into high gear, helping us make the moves necessary to avoid a crash. Many times, we are not even aware of what has happened, only that somehow our minds took the necessary steps to help us avoid a collision. We do not mind the jitters, sweating, and rapid heartbeat then!

When we step onstage to perform, our bodies are actually preparing for battle. Adrenaline is released into the bloodstream, our blood vessels and mucous membranes dilate, and our sinuses begin to drain—the same physiological responses. We sweat, we shake, our brain becomes otherwise engaged in self-protection, and we become distracted. We fumble for words and our performances suffer because of it.

Naturally, we want to find a way to eliminate these disturbing side effects, and therein lies the problem. We try to make our fears go away before a performance, when they are intended by nature to appear at exactly that moment. After all, imagine trying to calm down your body's adrenaline response in the face of a car crash.

Remember that your fears are on your side. The best thing to do when you experience stage fright is to embrace it, particularly since it is not going anywhere. Breathe into the fear, allow yourself to feel the shaking and nervousness and accept the rapid heartbeat. Your body is helping you gear up for a performance, and if you learn to embrace your stage fright and the corresponding physical reactions and to use them to your advantage, your performances will improve dramatically.

There are a number of techniques I use regarding stage fright that yield great results. When preparing for a performance, I have my clients either remember a past experience or visualize an upcoming event, causing the body to trigger the stage fright reactions. (Inviting their friends to lessons is also helpful, as is performing in a master class.) Before we work on how they will actually perform, I encourage them to sing through the piece while completely yielding to the stage fright, doing whatever the body instinctively wants to do, without qualification.

What happens next is fascinating. Rather than the vocal cracking and shaking, which come from attempts to suppress stage fright and fear, there is usually a lot of over-the-top expressiveness and loud singing. Because the adrenaline rush and corresponding effects are most powerful at their onset, this eventually settles down, producing a calmer, yet very intense, performance. The initial larger-than-life energy compresses to a powerful force that works beautifully to improve the performance.

By giving in and allowing the body to do what it wants to do instinctively, you come out a much more powerful and intense performer. This does not mean you need to tear up your dressing room before each show, but to participate actively in your performance and to perform well both depend on finding a way to embrace, rather than fight, the adrenaline rush.

Remember that your fears are on your side.

If my clients are having difficulty picturing performance conditions, I have them go for a run or consume some caffeine before a session, allowing the heartbeat to race and a sufficient sweat to develop. (I am not saying chugging three lattes is good for you, just that it can fabricate a comparable experience.) By artificially creating the physiological symptoms of anxiety, we are able to work through the repertoire of the performance under conditions similar to stage fright.

When the performance arrives, you can take additional steps to help integrate the nerves that are sure to come. Avoiding caffeine and other types of stimulants is a good first step, as their use only exacerbates the effects of stage fright and encourages dehydration. Eating lighter and smaller meals can also be beneficial, as large amounts of energy are required for digestion, thus reducing the amount of energy available for the performance. (Also, performing on an empty stomach reduces the likelihood of indigestion and acid reflux.) Making cardiovascular exercise a habit the day of a performance will help to reduce the heart rate after your workout session has concluded, encouraging breathing to relax and stress to be released from the muscles and mind. Of course, a regular exercise routine is highly beneficial for more relaxed and centered performances in general, and for the general health benefits of wellness: longevity, increased breath capacity, overall reduced stress levels, mental stability, and evenness of mood.

In addition to preparing for the initiation of stage fright, it is also imperative to prepare for its duration. You don't send out invitations months prior to a battle the way you announce an upcoming show. Attacks by their nature usually come out of the blue, thus the body's instantaneous and dramatic reaction. In performance however, you must expect that stage fright will come on strong and early, sometimes weeks and months in advance. Learn to allow this energy to empower rather than drain you as the performance date draws near, remembering not only that your fears come from within you, but that they are on your side.

The Studio Experience

For many of my clients, singing in a recording studio seems like a blessing, because their performance jitters are not usually present. While the absence of stage fright might seem comforting, it can cause its own set of problems. Without the crowd, the pressure to get it right the first time, and the excitement of a live performance, it is easy for some to get lazy.

Treat every recording session like a live performance.

Interestingly, the opposite also holds true. The lack of distractions and excitement causes a shift back into the technical mindset for many people, and the studio experience can be fraught with over-analysis, nervousness, and the compulsion to be perfect.[7] As we have seen before, when we allow our minds to get their "hands" on our voices, the result is always a shift in vocal production from the unconscious to the conscious, from the involuntary to the voluntary—both of which are usually for the worse.

My recommendation for achieving the best results in a studio setting is to treat every recording session like a live performance. If possible, go into your session believing that it is a live show, that you have one chance to really sell the song. If overdubs and edits are necessary, address them after the initial performance. Discuss with your engineers and producers beforehand that you would like to walk in and do a complete take or two, preferably at a predetermined time, to simulate a live situation as much as possible. Invite an audience if it will help you to create a performance environment. I have found that this practice tends to yield favorable results not only in performance quality, but also in emotional conviction and the "selling" of the song.

If you are able to "zen out" in the studio and prefer doing many different takes, then, with your team, create an environment that will allow you to foster this approach. Communicate in advance the way you would like to call takes and have cues called—as well as how you feel about headphone mixes, lighting, candles, and such—so that you do not have to snap out of the zone to tend to technical adjustments and issues.

The Live Experience

As we touched upon in the last chapter, performing live can throw even the most confident singer into a tailspin when the sound they consciously and unconsciously seek is lost as a result of a variance in acoustics or a poor monitor mix.

When I cannot hear myself well, I tend to sing off of my air without healthy, proper support in an effort to try to regain my audio and vocal frames of reference. This is actually the worst thing you can do. The natural reflex to hold back when you cannot hear well will result in a distortion of the way you produce sound, and will tend to flatten, thin, or strain your tone. Ironically, it is in this instance that you must temporarily ignore the wisdom of your fear and do your best to connect to a full and energized physical experience of singing. Concerns about the audio component can be addressed at the end of the performance.

Unless there are some major issues, the likelihood that the audio situation will dramatically affect your natural way of singing is small. This good news should alleviate the emotional and vocal apprehension that comes from an unfamiliar mix. It is more likely that you need to become comfortable with and adapt to singing with monitors. This takes time, and patience is required.

There are, however, various factors in a monitor mix that, when handled incorrectly, can distort the sound and cause major shifts in the way the voice is heard and sound produced (particularly with in-ear monitors).[8] If you find that you are darkening or nasalizing your tone, or that your voice is searching for pitch, or that you cannot hear yourself well (or at all), you may need to adjust the EQ[9] or compression[10] settings.

We get some great insight from recording engineer and producer Robert Wright:

> When the EQ and compression are right, you'll forget that you're listening to an electric reproduction of your voice, and muscle memory will adjust its link with the mind and interpret the monitor signal of your voice naturally and accordingly. But when the fundamental pitch suddenly disappears in the lower part of your range (an EQ problem) or when you sing a line with a mild crescendo while your monitor goes from a whisper to a bark (a compression problem), or worst of all, when you sing with everything you've got but your volume level never changes in your monitor (also a compression problem), you lose your bearings and start to drastically change your sound production. These mishaps also instill fear and apprehension—of damaging equipment, damaging your hearing, of looking "foolish" or inept—which robs you of the confidence responsible for communicating the intangibles of singing that make it an art.

While having the right settings is imperative for an ideal performance, Robert goes on to caution against the common mistake of opting for a pleasant sound over a predictable one:

> A lot of singers feel they will perform their best if what they hear from their monitor sounds polished and professional, sonically speaking. The truth is that the more smoothly your voice blends with the music, the broader your focus will become on what you are hearing, which means you will lose contact with the small details that need to be monitored closely during a performance. These include, but are not limited to: pitch, diction, vowel placement, timing/phrasing, breath support through long syllables and the intensity of your sound production (over- or under-singing). The better your voice blends into the sonic picture you hear from your monitor, the less capable you will be of singing your best, and you will not even be aware of it. It is when the voice is most clearly and legibly heard—think of a mild version of "sticking out like a sore thumb"—that you can hear the details that keep you in tune and in time.[11]

Other factors like microphone selection and technique, frequency masking,[12] panning,[13] and overall volume can also contribute to a good (or poor) sound situation. Learning as much as you can about the audio basics will not only help you become more fluent in the language of your trade, but will also help you to communicate more effectively to those around you what it is that you hear and need.

The Life Experience

Live singing and studio singing are not the only areas where the musician encounters fear. A wide range of decisions offstage needs to be made regarding how to handle your career and training (and life), and I believe that in these areas your fears can be the most helpful.

Becoming a singer is quite different than, for example, becoming a doctor. Get an undergraduate degree, take the MCAT entrance exam, attend medical school, and then do a residency and intership. Follow these steps successfully, and a doctor you will be. In performance, however, there is no right path, no right steps, and no guarantees that even the greatest of efforts will yield the desired result. It is this uncertainty that causes many people to allow frustration, delayed gratification, fear, and unpredictable income streams to stop them from following their dreams.

The reality, however, is that there are no guarantees in life. You can decide to choose a more secure path to avoid the stress and fears that come from bolder ambitions. However, that choice will not guarantee that you will not be fired, disbarred, downsized, sued for malpractice, or encounter an unexpected situation that will prevent you from performing in a more reliable career. From this point of view, what is the purpose of "playing it safe"?

The only real option for achieving true success and fulfillment in life is to know what you want and to trust yourself, keeping hard work, determination, integrity, a positive attitude, and an open mind as your trademarks. Let the fear you feel about your dreams and the decisions you've made and need to make act as helpful markers for how to proceed, rather than as constant roadblocks. After all, it takes far less energy to decide to try a new approach or to do something new than to spend years agonizing over whether or not you have made good decisions.

Obtaining guidance from those with experience in your chosen field can be priceless, especially in the artistic realm where there is not a set path to follow. Still, while many offer sage advice regarding career advancement, it is easy to allow fear to facilitate the development of unhealthy, co-dependent relationships with people filled with promises of how they will cut you a break or make you a star. Even those with the best intentions may have less-than-ideal ideas about how you should approach your dream, and it is tempting to rely on them when you are unsure of yourself. Instead, take time to get to know who you are and to discover what it is you truly want, so that you can feel confident that you are on the right path for the right reasons. When you have that confidence, it will be easier to choose which incoming information to embrace, and which to discard.

As I mentioned in the first chapter, I was shocked to learn from my first university coach that all forms of singing other than the classical approach were incorrect. A part of me knew this could not be true, but I chose instead to trust an "expert opinion" over my own intuition.

Learn to trust your instincts. They will rarely steer you wrong.

This is also important when it comes to vocal and general health. Like teachers, doctors often have differing opinions on how best to handle and care for your body and voice. The number of rehabilitative options exhausted before the suggestion of surgery varies from doctor to doctor, though in my experience and opinion, the latter is suggested far too often and far too soon.

The bottom line is this: If something does not feel right, it probably is not, regardless of what your doctor, coach, boss, manager, or agent may be telling you. Carefully and patiently search out second and third opinions if you feel uncertain of any advice you receive. And once again, learn to trust your instincts. They will rarely steer you wrong.

Chapter 7

Putting Theory Into Practice

About halfway through reading an early manuscript of this book, a music producer friend of mine asked, "When are you going to get to the part about singing?"

It is very easy—and common—to begin, fill, and end a conversation about voice production with talk of technique and exercises, and indeed here and in the accompanying CD we will explore various tools that will help you to physically manifest your best voice.

Still, a technical knowledge is beneficial only if a natural understanding has been fostered, and practicing without a true survey and understanding of what we have discussed so far can actually do more harm than good. A Broadway client comes to mind who, after years of adherence to strictly technical training and practice, was stunned to watch her voice skyrocket to new levels after considering and implementing the "non-vocal" elements we've discussed thus far.

The Truth About Technique

Do not conquer the world with force, for force only causes resistance.[1]

—Lao Tsu

Learning technique has become a clinical, uncertain, and literally out-of-body experience for many people, one that demands the extension of yourself toward a foreign, complicated set of tools and understandings that you currently do not and cannot inherently possess.

The reality, however, is quite different. Technique, in both healthy practice and by definition, is not an external goal, but rather "the manner in which technical details are treated (as by a writer) or basic physical movements are used (as by a dancer); AND: the ability to treat such details or use such movements: a method of accomplishing a desired aim."[2]

You will note that this definition assumes that these details are not only already possessed, but are under the command and direction of the one possessing that technique. The singer is empowered and in charge, not the technique. Thus, the idea of technique, while certainly involving knowledge acquisition, is, in practice, about empowered and integrated implementation (the "treating" and "using") of what we already know and have learned—from the inside, out.

The Four C's

I find that the best way to approach technique is to focus less on how you are implementing a vocal action (as often we cannot describe the experience or explain the process), and more on whether or not you are obtaining certain results. Singing is an experience of experiencing, and in your role as empowered witness rather than anxious controller, the Four C's—the ability to sing Consistently, Creatively, Comfortably, and on-Command—are correctly positioned to let you observe whether or not you are on the right track.

Having a **consistent** voice means that, regardless of your health, emotional state, level of fatigue, stress, and similar variables, your body and mind have reached an unconscious and reflexive understanding of how to allow the voice to engage and make the tiny adjustments necessary in breath, support, and musculature to compensate for any vocal distraction.

Creative singing implies that you are able to sing in a variety of styles and ranges with varying degrees of volume, emotion, resonance, and intensity. If you are the greatest Broadway belter in the world but have no head voice to speak of, you are straining your chest tone at the expense of your head voice and register shifts. While this approach (which is not necessary to achieve powerful, high chest tones) might lead to a beautiful sound in certain styles and registers, it cannot be **comfortable**, certainly not on a regular basis, so neither the second nor the third requirement has been met.

No matter where you currently are, the distance from there to singing well is not as far as you might imagine.

While similar to singing consistently, being **on-command** touches on a very distinct issue. You could have a pinched throat and still sing very consistently, meaning that you have learned how to manipulate your tone, delivery, and musculature in a way that allows the voice to regularly achieve a similar and predictable result. However, unless you are singing in a natural and relaxed way, you are going to have a hard time using your voice on-command… at any moment, for any length of time.

If you have three of the four C's, you are not there. A consistent, comfortable, and on-command voice, if it cannot be creative in its use, is usually undeveloped in certain areas. Your voice might be creatively brilliant and resonant, but something is surely wrong if, after an hour of singing, you are fatigued and have vocal strain. However, if your voice is reliable at any time and for any period of time, and is always able to comfortably and flexibly approach any kind of material, range, and volume, you are almost certainly creating sound in a way that is in line with the healthy use of your vocal mechanism.

If you have spent years being "not quite there" (or not there at all), or if you are new to singing, where to begin? Just as preferences for learning and processing information vary, so should each individual's strategy. But no matter where you currently are, the distance from there to singing well is not as far as you might imagine.

The Truth About Practice

Break the chains of your thought, and you break the chains of your body, too.[3]
—Richard Bach

- Correct practice yields correct outcomes.
- Poor practice, no matter how frequent, will only reinforce bad habits.
- The mind, rather than the body, requires the greatest amount of attention and diligence in practice.
- Practice need not be conventional to be practice.

Practice Doesn't Make Perfect

There is a famous saying: "Practice makes perfect," though in my opinion it is more accurately stated as, "Correct practice leads to correct outcomes, while incorrect practice leads to further ingrained bad habits."

If you are singing incorrectly, practicing three hours a day will not improve your voice. In fact, it will serve only to further reinforce bad habits, both physical and mental. Still, people waste time using quantity of practice over quality of practice in an effort to achieve mastery of the voice. Why? Because engrained bad habits do not seem to want to dissipate with minimal practice. Add a prevalent cultural work ethic that says more is better, and the result is hours of frequently non-constructive, and many times harmful, practice.

People waste time using quantity of practice over quality of practice.

Instead of practicing often, practice smart. Rather than striving for technical perfection in both outcome and form, strive in approach and comprehension for predictability and comfort. If your practice is not yielding the results you want, consider that it might be the type or method of your practice that is problematic, rather than the amount of time spent.

Mind-Over-Body Education

Smart practice begins with the mind rather than the voice. Regardless of what the body knows, the mind hears the language of singing and affects the musculature accordingly. It is the mind that thinks a big, beautiful song requires a big and not-so-beautiful amount of tension. It is the mind that allows fear, uncertainty, and insecurity to control the physical outcome. The body gives up its right to comfort and ease when the mind demands reconciliation with preconceived notions, ingrained habits, and non-integrated training. As we have been discussing, all the scales and exercises in the world will not counteract a mind that is inhibiting its own ability to process and manifest information optimally.

It is mind that thinks a big, beautiful song requires a big and not-so-beautiful amount of tension.

When I first met Maria, I was not sure I would be able to help her achieve her goal of becoming a truly incredible singer. While she had years of training under her belt, her voice was tight and easily fatigued, even when speaking. There were glimpses of freedom and hints of tonal beauty, but I decided to work with her more for her passion than for a hope of unleashing the world's greatest vocalist.

I love sharing this story, not only because it brings me so much joy, but also because it is so encouraging. Maria not only proved my theory of the mind's power over the physical voice, she also proved me wrong.

With careful and extremely patient practice, Maria was able to allow her voice to emerge from under the mental and physical rigidity that had been literally locking her instrument away. Within a year, she not only became truly one of the best singers I have ever worked with, but a great communicator in a variety of musical styles. She has surpassed my abilities technically as a singer, and gives me goose bumps (and often makes me cry) in an increasing number of sessions.

Clearly, some of Maria's vocal growth has come from physical training, from nurturing and developing her physical strength and vocal body. But the majority of her awesome progress has been due to releasing the mental strongholds and corresponding physical tensions that had been blocking an instrument waiting there, largely developed, all along.

A correct physical action performed even one time is recorded in your body's muscle memory, and an open mind that is prepared to allow, observe, and experience correct physical action will be receptive to making that action a habit. That correct action repeated carefully, that correct mentality fostered gently, will result in leading the voice and mind to the healthy space where natural, instinctive, and integrated vocal development live.

Shaking Off Convention

As training is in large part about the mind, it is imperative to provide for it a comfortable and safe environment. Because of past experiences, performance anxiety, or preconceived notions, many people become nervous upon entering a practice room or recording studio. In this case, I say avoid these places. Nothing says you cannot learn as well in the shower as in a rehearsal space. In fact, singing in the shower or in the car while your mind is otherwise engaged can actually be the ideal situation for distracting the technical inhibitors and allowing the natural voice to emerge. Done often enough, muscle memory shapes these natural actions into habit, at which point the distractions can be removed and the voice consciously explored further.

Focus on your personal preferences and comfort. Find a place where you feel relaxed. Training (that is, observing, developing, and conditioning the intuitive process of singing) done in a comfortable setting will help facilitate a correct frame of mind. Whether you prefer to run scales in a rehearsal room or to sing your favorite songs during your morning commute, it is comfort and conscious attention to vocal production rather than structure of practice that will best help you achieve your goals.

Nothing says you cannot learn as well in the shower as in a rehearsal space.

The advantages of not singing are endless in vocal training as well. Consider and monitor the effortlessness of your breath and speaking voice. Monitor yourself as you think about singing, and prepare to sing. Listen to recordings of different singers in various styles. Attend concerts, master classes, and rehearsals. Many times we are not aware of our vocal and mental habits, only to realize them when we see them manifesting in others. Observation, as we discussed in chapter five, is invaluable to your voice education.

The Five S's

Regardless of where you are on the scales from beginner to expert, from confused to certain, or from technical to intuitive, there are certain fundamentals that I have found to be highly beneficial for every singer I have worked with. We will discuss these concepts and walk through the basics of each that you can then build upon on your own and with trusted friends and coaches. The accompanying CD will lead us on this journey, with discussion and musical notation of the exercises found in the corresponding sections below. If you are a visual or aural learner, perhaps begin with the book or CD exclusively, later using them in conjunction with one another for a broader explanation and understanding.

Before we get started, I want to emphasize again that developing your voice is first a process of observation rather than implementation. It does not begin with engaging muscles and mindsets; it begins with letting them go. Be a witness first and an instrument of fine-tuning second and your singing will not only improve dramatically, but will become effortless and enjoyable.

Sip

I have never been extremely sensitive to food or drink when it comes to singing. I love cheese, drink too much coffee, and enjoy a glass of wine now and again. While I notice the effects they can have on my voice, they are not significant enough for me to think of making a change.

General and pre-singing diets affect some people more than others, and obviously, you need to discover what works best for you. But when it comes to hydration, I cannot stress enough my belief in its importance, both for general health and for that of the vocal mechanism.

If you are a singer, I strongly encourage you to drink a lot of water, all the time.[4] Do not just drink water the morning of a gig or coaching—there will not be enough time for the water to hydrate the tissues and flush the system—but all the time. I could give you scores of examples of how sessions, performances, and even voices have succeeded and failed based on this one variable. Water is truly a singer's best friend.

When you are well-hydrated, your vocal folds are agile and fresh. The membranes around them are limber and clear. The mucous is thin and well-drained, not only in your throat, but in your ears as well, resolving minor pitch discrepancies caused by congestion. The arytenoids can move effortlessly, and the sinus passages are clear and lubricated, allowing sound and resonance to travel easily. The vocal mechanism finds a consistent center, and strength and vocal training can proceed in a predictable and healthy fashion. The mind is less inclined to headaches and fuzziness, promoting alertness. The body functions better in every way.[5]

> *When you are not well-hydrated, the body needs to work harder to produce sound.*

When you are not well-hydrated, the body needs to work harder to produce sound. Muscles overcompensate for thick vocal cords and a sluggish mechanism, often causing stress and tension. Congestion leads to the temptation of throat clearing and coughing, both potentially detrimental. Without hydration, you are more susceptible to colds and viruses. Your immune system is more vulnerable. Your skin is not as clear.

Have your cappuccino, drink some red wine with dinner, enjoy the occasional martini with friends. I am not going to tell you to become a saint, but I will tell you to drink as much water as possible, especially if you are into caffeine, dairy, or alcohol—or, heaven forbid, cigarettes. Enjoy your life—and drink lots of water. Find a way to make it a habit.

Strengthen

The most important aspect of physical vocal development is the strengthening and connecting of the support mechanism to voice production. To use a metaphor, a building is only as stable as the foundation upon which it stands, and the same holds true for your voice. Before you can do any developmental work on power, agility, or register shifts, you must first have the foundation of the breath support securely in place.

The Diaphragm

This support system revolves largely around a muscle called the diaphragm. The diaphragm is a sheet of muscle that rests under your lungs and rib cage, and, on command from the brain, works in conjunction with the lungs to enable respiration. Though we cannot actively engage the diaphragm,[6] it has been receiving around-the-clock training with every breath we have taken since we were born.

Awareness of the Diaphragm

The following two exercises will help you to develop an awareness of your diaphragm. Try them both a few times and observe what you feel:

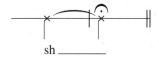

While every person will experience the diaphragm differently, the sensation you are looking for is something like a tightening or contraction somewhere near the stomach.[7] The more breath you exhale and the harder you do so, the more tension you are bound to feel in that region. This is your diaphragm and its related musculature at work, and the process of healthy vocal development begins with the awareness and strengthening these powerful muscles.[8]

> *Witness what the body does and wants to do naturally and on its own.*

Because we are not meeting face to face, I have to describe common sensations of the diaphragm, but remember that it is much more important to focus on whatever sensations you personally may experience. This includes what you may not feel; do not force yourself to try to find a feeling that is in alignment with what I am describing here or a technical understanding of how the diaphragm and breath supposedly operate. Often it takes time to become aware of sensations that you have never focused on or been in tune with before. Not only do we all experience breath support differently, factors like hydration, fatigue, and stress will further vary the sensations. This is all the more reason to allow your body to engage the support on its own, rather than try to look for a preconceived sensation.

This may be difficult for those of you who have been singing for a while, and in particular, those with training and coaching experience. Many of you have focused so much on consciously trying to engage the diaphragm that standing back and observing the process will be a challenge. Resist the urge to become actively involved and instead, witness what the body does and wants to do naturally and on its own.

Strengthening the Diaphragm

Extension

Once you feel a sense of connection, play around a bit with some of the following variations, all of which you can also do on an "s" sound:

 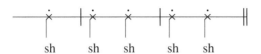

 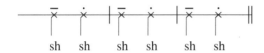

 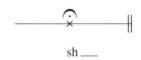

These exercises will not only help you become acquainted with the sensations of the diaphragm in different contexts, but will start to tone and strengthen the muscle, preparing you for getting to work on connecting it to voice production. These four exercises are particularly helpful, as in many ways they mimic the use of the diaphragmatic musculature in singing: in well-articulated lines, in emotionally expressive and varied ones, and in long-held tones, respectively.

Non-Voiced Consonants

Another way to experience the diaphragm is in the use of explosive, non-voiced consonants, such as P, T, K, and F. Given that many of the words we speak and sing begin with these letters, their use as an exercise not only helps to draw our attention to the diaphragm's role in producing these sounds, but to link the speaking and singing processes in our minds and, more importantly, in our bodies:

 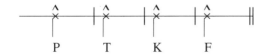

You may not be aware of the support mechanism in your daily speech, so feel free to vary and play with volume and intensity in this exercise. In fact, exaggeration—but not forcing—of all of the strengthening exercises should help to increase your conscious awareness of the muscle as well as to develop it.

Lip trills

Another, though slightly messier, exercise to engage and strengthen the diaphragm is the lip trill, accomplished by blowing air through your lips while keeping them—along with your face and neck—relaxed.

(non-voiced) Brrr _____

Compared with the previous "sh" and "s" exercises, there is more opportunity here for unhealthy tension. Aside from occasional complications due to structure of the lips and mouth, this exercise more clearly exposes troubles caused or exacerbated by a disconnected support, which tend to show up in the singing as well. This usually results in an inconsistent lip trill, or a thinner-sounding one with a higher timbre. A glance in the mirror can also reveal issues with the support process; the pursing of lips, high and tight breathing, and/or dimpling of the chin and cheeks are visual signs of troubles you may not be able to hear.

What you are looking for is a nice, relaxed engagement, clearly felt in the area of the diaphragm, with no tension in the face. If you are having trouble, it is often helpful to begin engaging a lip trill in the midst of an exhalation, a practice you can use with all of the strengthening exercises, as well as many we will explore in the next sections:

exhale __ Brrr _____(non-voiced)

When relaxed and free, holding a consistent and extended lip trill not only works to strengthen and tone the diaphragm, but to practice physically and mentally keeping the breath fully engaged throughout a phrase. Often the mind, in hearing a delicately sung line, tries incorrectly to match the phrase with an equally delicate engagement and support of air. The breath needs to remain strong even in the quietest of singing, as well as through the ends of phrases. Singers often lose their mental focus as a phrase comes to a close, which manifests in the diminishing of breath support and the weakening of a quality vocal performance. The lip trill helps to alter these associations.

In addition to the extended lip trill, you can also vary the duration of and approach to this exercise as we did on tracks 5, 6, 7, and 8. This will serve to further strengthen your diaphragm, as well as bring increased and expanded awareness to its functioning.

Inhalation

You will notice that I have said nothing about breathing, nor about "proper inhalation." Even if you were actively thinking about taking a breath before each exercise, you most likely were not conscious of the one you took after you finished. Your mind and body coordinated to replenish your air automatically, as they always do, and the witnessing of this automatic process is crucial.

Try exhaling as much air as possible on a "sh" sound, then do all you can to avoid a deliberate inhalation. Observe how your body naturally takes in air. Where do you feel this? If you are truly relaxed, the sensation will be lower in the torso rather than in the upper chest and lower throat where it is for many people who actively try to engage—and in many ways interfere with—their breathing.

For those of you who have had a lot of training, the desire to intentionally inhale will remain a strong one—one that will take patience and practice to resist. Once you are able to experience a natural inhalation, it is helpful for many of my trained singers to take the "deep, active breath" they are used to after a full exhalation on a "sh." This usually helps them become acutely aware of any tension they are adding when they deliberately try to inhale, and therefore encourages them to let it go.

Subglottal Pressure

The strengthening of the diaphragm and breath support is directly connected to something called subglottal pressure. In simple terms, this pressure is what keeps the upward force of the exhalation from the lungs balanced and healthy, so that the voice is safely buoyed on a correctly pressurized amount of air. The ability to maintain (note that I did not say "control") the balance of this pressure is the key to keeping the sensations of openness and relaxation in the throat. Like healthy breathing and diaphragmatic engagement, it is largely involuntary, though dramatically affected by both positive and negative tension utilized in the vocal production process.

As an example, think of the open, relaxed, and natural voice of Frank Sinatra as compared with one of today's powerhouse, high-belting country or pop singers. The country or pop singer's desire to achieve an emotional sound is often at the expense of both a relaxed, open throat and appropriate subglottal pressure. Not only is it unnecessary to strain or compromise this pressure to achieve a powerful-sounding tone (air, rather than tension, is the correct "emotion-maker"), if over-utilized, this approach can cause problems with the health of the vocal folds.

Another practice that often interferes with a healthy subglottal pressure is the taking of excessively deep breaths or forcibly trying to "expand out" to create room for them. When too much air is deliberately inhaled and essentially held in waiting—in the common effort to "prepare it"[9]— the air can become incorrectly pressurized both before and as it is released, causing tension in the voice box.

As a point of reference, I experience subglottal pressure in conjunction with the upward kick of the diaphragm's contraction, as a slightly downward sensation starting in the area of my sternum.[10] (Many people are not aware of subglottal pressure at all, particularly in the beginning of their vocal development.) The two result in a completely wide-open and tension-free feeling in my throat when I speak. There is no sensation of lifting, and there is absolutely no tension in my neck, shoulders, or face. When I sing, I feel this same combination of sensations in greater and varying intensity. There are times in vocal training when it is helpful to consciously focus on and manage the balance of these two pressures, but always remembering and building upon the natural relationship.

Conditioning Awareness of the Support Mechanism

While we are ready to move on, I recommend that you return to the Strengthen section periodically, especially at the beginning of your vocal training. The mind and body learn differently. It is therefore important not only to intellectually understand the concept and mechanics of breath support, but also to allow your body and muscle memory time to experience, internalize, and make a habit of its proper use. Moving forward will be much easier once this has been achieved.

Some of my new clients leave sessions a bit confused or frustrated when I tell them that these and similar exercises are the only ones they are to work on for a couple of weeks. They are determined to do some kind of singing, whether running scales or working through a song, certain that progress can come only once the singing voice is engaged. I tell them what I now tell you: without the benefit of these exercises quite literally under your belt, your singing will not be able to be developed optimally. My clients who choose to be disciplined with this approach are grateful for the benefits and exponential growth that soon follow.

Speak

Like breathing, most of us speak every day without a conscious thought. Our goal in this section is not to change that in any way, but to observe and become aware of what is going on in our bodies and minds when we talk, so that we can relate the experience to singing.

This connection, which is actually a reconnection, is crucial for vocal success. The common divide between singing and speaking is more psychological than physiological, which manifests in a host of physical tensions that then reaffirm this incorrect view. By developing awareness of our natural speech without affecting it in any way, we can make a conscious mental habit of the intuitive physical process, and with enough conditioning, transfer this approach to singing with similar results.

Awareness in Daily Speech

Start by bringing your conscious attention to things you say every day. Whether you want to say something out loud now or pay attention the next time you run into a friend, focus on what it feels like to speak common phrases such as, "How are you?" "What's going on?" or "Hey, there!"

This experience may feel strange for some of you, as you are trying to pay attention to a process of which you are rarely—if ever—aware. This sense of confusion is the result of actively trying to engage the technical mind in a wholly intuitive process, and, in the long term, we hope to be able to experience this connection with the intuitive process—free from the technical mind—with singing as well.

Taking this a step further, play around with the volume, intensity, and way you speak these and other common phrases, and see if they feel any different. See if you can observe how your speech begins with the support structure, passes through the body, and leaves your mouth as a spoken tone. How are you creating these sounds? How are you accomplishing these modifications?

By now, I hope you realize that I am not looking for concrete answers, or answers at all. The moves and changes we make with our speaking voices—regardless of how big they sound—are generated by simple and often unconscious thoughts, rather than by direct intention or manipulation of musculature. What I am trying to do instead, as we discussed in chapter five, is to get you to become aware that while you may not know how you are speaking, or how you are modifying your voice and breath, this does not mean that you are not completely knowledgeable and in charge of the process. This is extremely important as we proceed; just because we cannot verbally explain how we produce sound does not mean that we do not understand what is going on. We just understand in a non-conscious, non-technical, and non-linguistic way.

Non-Voiced to Voiced Consonants

Let's build upon an example from the previous section. After going through the non-voiced consonants P, T, S, and F with attention to any sensation in the area of diaphragm, let's shift to their voiced counterparts B, D, Z, and V:[11]

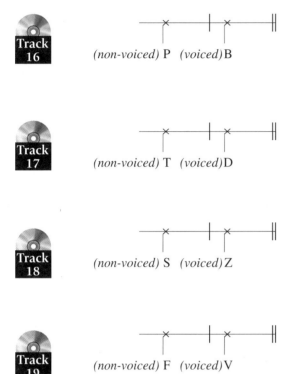

Track 16 — (non-voiced) P (voiced) B

Track 17 — (non-voiced) T (voiced) D

Track 18 — (non-voiced) S (voiced) Z

Track 19 — (non-voiced) F (voiced) V

Voiced Consonants to Speech

Using the non-voiced consonants P, T, K, and F, add on the following words, remembering that the goal of these exercises is observation rather than engagement:

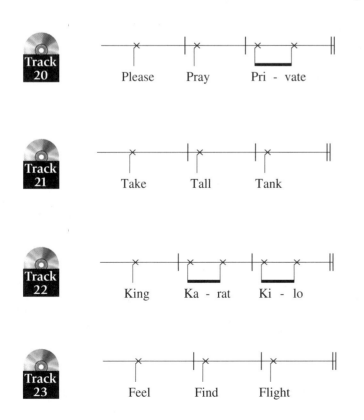

Track 20 — Please   Pray   Pri - vate

Track 21 — Take   Tall   Tank

Track 22 — King   Ka - rat   Ki - lo

Track 23 — Feel   Find   Flight

Let's also add words corresponding to the first exercises we looked at together:

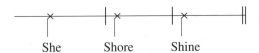

She   Shore   Shine

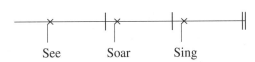

See   Soar   Sing

By bringing conscious attention to speaking these words, our technical minds will often try to get involved, altering the natural way we say and/or experience them. When you feel confident that you are actually observing your speech, rather than affecting the breath or voice in any way, try these exercises again and see if you notice any difference or change in sensation as you move between non-voiced consonants and their voiced counterparts. Do you notice any shifts in physical sensation when you add words to the non-voiced consonants. If so, where do you experience them?

Voiced Lip Trills

Building upon another exercise from the Strengthen section, add voice—spoken, not sung—to the lip trill. Begin mid-exhalation again, if you would like:

(voiced) Brrr _____

Take note of how you experience the difference between a non-voiced and voiced lip trill, if at all. Also, watch yourself in a mirror to make sure that the only additional element you are engaging is your voice, rather than a host of physical tensions. While I cannot tell you what specific variations in feeling you will notice, I can tell you that any differences should be minimal. It is a mental signal more than any additional muscular engagement that causes the vocal folds to come together and vibrate, and the voice to resonate, when the shift is made from a non-voiced to voiced lip trill.

Speech as a Transition to Song

Once you feel that you have truly observed and internalized the sensations of what we have gone through so far, let's move on to one of my favorite building blocks in voice production, which we will greatly expand upon in the next section. Try saying (not singing) the alphabet aloud from start to finish, going as far as you can on a single breath:

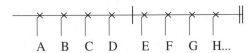

A   B   C   D   E   F   G   H...

Try it a few times, and as with all of the other exercises, vary it a bit by using different volumes and expressions. Do you feel the diaphragm engage more as you progress, if at all? How do the letters feel being formed in your mouth and as they leave? If you did not make it all the way through on a single breath, can you remember when you started running out of air? Do you recall when you breathed, and what that breath felt like?

Another exercise I want to suggest is to speak through a song's lyric. Like the alphabet, which we associate with a memorable melody, simply reading or reciting lyrics can cause the mind to activate apprehension and musculature that will accompany its vocalization. Thus, it is a particularly helpful exercise before working through a piece, one that can preemptively demonstrate both the physical and mental tensions that may lie ahead.

As we discussed in chapter five, the "song" of speech is found in the intuitive mind, and so approaching anything remotely involving singing engages the technical mind's inhibitions. Therefore, try to remove the idea of the song when speaking through a lyric and simply say the words, as though placing an order at a restaurant. An affected voice and breath immediately shift to effortless and liberated speech. Experiment on your own and see if you can hear—and, more importantly, feel—the differences in your own voice and body.

Once you are able to freely speak lyrics you are working on, begin to play with the way you "sing" the spoken word. Enjoy the way the language leaves your lips and your ability to affect emotion. This step can be challenging, as the brain wrestles with whether or not it is singing or speaking and which corresponding tensions to engage or release.

Our goal, of course, is to streamline the two experiences, so that the most passionate communication, sung or spoken, triggers the same mental and physical engagement as regular speech. Psychologically, you may be convinced that attaching lyrics to pre-designated notes will somehow physically complicate the matter. Psychologically, you may become nervous at the idea of feeling vulnerable or emotionally exposed in the sung version, which can affect the way you produce sound. But none of this changes the fact that, physiologically, the processes are by nature virtually the same. Volume, inflection, and even certain notes occur in your speech; you are just not consciously aware of or trying to engage them. If we can get our minds to accept and believe that they are the same, we will begin to create a healthy space where beautiful singing is no more intellectually complicated or stressful than speaking.

Sing

Making the Transition

The challenge, of course, is getting this idea manifested in your body, so that it may be believed by your mind. For many, singing is not only a completely separate experience from speaking, but one laden with fear and tension. We will therefore continue walking slowly along our bridge from speech to song, always keeping one foot in the former, until we arrive at the latter with your technical mind none the wiser.

We will do this by making this bridge tangible. By expanding on the tools and exercises with which we have already succeeded in the speaking section, we will strengthen our mental and physical assurance in the intuitive process. The technical mind will not sense that a transition between speech and song is actually occurring until it has already happened, thus preventing mental resistance and unnecessary physical engagement. Muscle memory will record the intuitive method of vocal production, and carefully nurtured and repeated, it will become a habit.

Engaging the Singing Voice

We will start out by going back to the alphabet exercise. Keep the same focus you had, in the speech section, on not engaging your breath consciously, as well as staying conversational. Observe the sensations you experience in your body as you speak through the entire alphabet (at a relatively good speed) on these notes:[12]

A B C D E F G H I J K L M N O P Q R S T U V double-U X Y Z

If you are like most of my clients, you likely have a puzzled expression on your face right now. This is the look of a confused technical mind unable to make sense of this strange assignment. By first dissociating the alphabet from a familiar melody and then linking it to a new one, hopefully we so overwhelmed the technical mind that it forgot to monitor and inhibit the exercise, allowing the natural voice to emerge long enough for you to experience singing as it should be. While you may feel dazed and confused, the intuitive mind and body are totally alert and storing these positive sensations in your muscle memory.

Vocal Integration

This is our first truly great chance to discover whether or how much our singing and speaking voices are separate from one another. Did you feel comfortable with this exercise, or did it seem completely foreign from what you call singing? Did your mind start to panic—or is it panicking now—at the inability to control this new approach to the alphabet? In asking you to consider the experience, I am not asking you to try to physically recreate it; the technical mind wants nothing more than a chance to go back, participate in, and manipulate what it somehow missed moments ago. Do not give it the chance.

Thirds and Fifths

Try the previous exercise again, this time integrating regular speech every four notes, making sure to keep both conversational:

A B C D E F G H I J K L M N O P Q R S T U V double-U X Y Z

If you did not feel confused a minute ago, you probably do now. Again, not giving your technical mind a chance to catch up, change the game once more, moving from an interval of a third to that of a fifth:

A B C D E F G H I J K L M N O P Q R S T U V double-U X Y Z

Vary the volume and intensity of the approach. Also, immediately repeat the alphabet once you get to the end. Observe what these longer phrases do to your breath, and how your body replenishes air. Now start on the fifth, and see if you notice any difference:

A B C D E F G H I J K L M N O P Q R S T U V double-U X Y Z

Did you feel any resistance from your mind or body at the suggestion of starting on a "high" note? Did that change the experience for you in any way? If you feel stuck or find that your technical mind is trying to get its "hands" back on your voice, always feel free to re-integrate speech to re-strengthen the proper connection:

A B C D E F G H I J K L M N O P Q R S T U V double-U X Y Z

Comprehension

Without trying the exercises again, pause for a moment to consider all of what you just experienced. Remember, your technical mind is not going to understand this in a way that it would like. You did not "understand" how your diaphragm engaged. You did not "understand" how you spoke. You did not "understand" how you varied the expression and the sound of emotion in your speech. What makes you think singing is somehow going to be different?

You will understand how you are able to sing, but it is going to be through observation and recognition of sensations that will become familiar and consistent over time, rather than by owning the knowledge in a technical and conscious way. Many of you may be uncomfortable with this approach, but by choosing to remain in the technical mind and not accessing the intuitive one fully, you will limit the scope and range of your abilities as singer.

To demonstrate this concept, hold out your left hand and, with your right, smack it as hard as you can four or five times. (If you are left-handed, reverse the process.) Do not hurt yourself, but make it sting a little. Now run your index finger as lightly as possible over the same area of skin. You may feel this, but the sensation is probably not too clear because of the remaining sting, as well as the contrast between such a light touch and the much more intense one that preceded it.

When you are used to the abrupt and hands-on way that most of us have experienced the rigid, conscious, technical engagement of the voice, the intuitive approach is going to feel like a light breeze going by: something you barely feel or notice, if at all. But if you stop the smacking (that is, the forcing and manipulation), the gentle and tiny caresses of your finger will eventually become as loud and intense as the smack, and you will begin to feel the subtleties in each one.

> *You achieve it by letting go, and by being willing to experience singing as you experience speaking and breathing: as an effortless experience without conscious control.*

This is what singing—like speaking, like breathing—will feel like in its correct place. You cannot achieve it by trying to manage individual engagements and manipulations. You achieve it by letting go, and by being willing to experience singing as you experience speaking and breathing: as an effortless experience without conscious control. A world of sensation lives in the gentle caress of the intuitive vocal process, which will, in time and through awareness, become incredibly rich and varied.

Lyrics

Using the same approach we took with the alphabet at the beginning of this section, let's now shift to the lyric of a song. Using "Amazing Grace" as an example, focus on saying the words conversationally without regard to emotion or performance:

A - ma - zing grace, how sweet the sound, that saved a wretch like me.

Do not worry if you stumble a bit or feel completely lost. Just move forward, not worrying about the sound or emotion as you continue concentrating on saying the words conversationally:

I once was lost, but now am found, was blind, but now I see.

How did you create these sounds? How did you move between the three, and then five, notes? Did you feel a difference? Do not answer by allowing your technical mind to try it again. Instead, observe whatever it is you felt and are feeling, and take note of this way of experiencing of singing.

Many variations on this theme work beautifully to confuse the technical mind while conditioning the intuitive vocal connection. One I find particularly useful is to have clients use the same three- or five-note configuration to communicate whatever it is they want to say to me in conversation. As you progress, you can jazz up, expand the range and inflection of the "exercise" to experience and develop different aspects of the voice, as well as strengthen the connection between speech and song.

Vibrato

For those of you new to singing, vibrato is a sound created by air passing through the vocal cords on sustained notes. On the CD, I demonstrate this on Track 38 and further discuss and demonstrate the vibrato on Track 39.

The vibrato is no more advanced than anything we have discussed so far, and certainly is not something that you consciously want to try to create. Like diaphragmatic engagement and like the achievement of certain pitches, a healthy vibrato occurs naturally, and is the sign of an open throat with a correctly pressurized amount of air flowing through. New students who have had trouble with their vibratos stumble upon them completely unintentionally once they have strengthened the support mechanism, relaxed corresponding throat tension, and released the idea of creating a specific sound.

This does not mean that a voice without vibrato is unhealthy, or not as open. Many great singers straighten out their vibratos deliberately for artistic effect. On the other hand, some singers have a vibrato that either warbles, or is longer and wider in its pattern of vibration. Sometimes a singer will have a vibrato like this throughout the range, and other times it will be in a specific area of the voice or around certain register shifts. In my experience, this kind of vibrato is usually the result of a tremendous amount of tension from pushing or contorting the voice in some way. (I find this often in belters and gospel singers.) The fact that it is usually a vocal manifestation caused by musculature, rather than a function of the structure of the vocal cords, is good news, and means that with the correct approach and discipline you can retrain the muscles and breath to allow the cords to vibrate in a healthy way.

Conditioning the Speech-to-Song Connection

As we prepare to move on, let's revisit the lip trill to tie together what we have done in terms of strengthening the speech-to-song transition. Starting at the beginning, move through the various stages, from non-voiced, to voiced, to a single note, to a third, and then to a fifth. You can of course later expand upon this exercise in a variety of ways, always being careful to ensure that the sound and quality of the lip trill remain essentially consistent throughout:

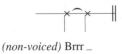

(non-voiced) Brrr   (voiced) Brrr   Brrr   Brrr   Brrr

Stylize

In my studio, stylization is the most exciting part of training, not only because vocal beauty and individuality really start to emerge, but also because true playing with the voice can finally begin. Clients by this time have transitioned back to the intuitive mode of singing, so the expansion and development of their voices come with a sense of wonder and excitement, which of course is a joy for them and for me.

At this point, it no longer seems ironic that the most audible aspects of the vocal development (flexibility, range, ring, and power) are actually the most effortless, both to experience and to develop into habit. Much like the vibrato that we talked about moments ago, they all come once a healthy mindset and a strong and conditioned support mechanism are in place. Singers who enter my studio with a technical determination to improve their voices always reach this stage in a state of amazement. Instead of incremental results through a prescribed training regime, they usually randomly stumble upon advanced vocalization and improved sound with a shake of the head and a casual smile. They never would have guessed that this is what the development of technique feels like, and yet it feels right.

This is true not only in a singer's typical genre, but in others as well. Many of my rock and pop clients started off convinced that Broadway and classical singing exist in totally different realms from the ones in which they make their living, and my classical singers at first could not imagine that they could sing R&B riffs or create a true belt sound. But at this level, resonance, register shifts, placement, coloring, texturing, runs, trills, and turns—in all styles of music—are possible with a well-supported and consistently engaged instrument, coupled with a sense of relaxed experimentation and a willingness to play.

A great deal of work and training goes into developing and polishing many a voice, but do not forget how many singers of the highest ability and esteem have never had a singing lesson in their lives. Instinct and intuition guide them, as they are meant to guide us all, toward optimal vocal performance and expression.

Hearing vs. Feeling

At this point, it is also no longer ironic to watch how advanced singers experience the sound of their voices. When we first meet, they are determined to monitor and hear every note and inflection. You might think this desire would only get stronger the more they progress, the more a liberated and exciting voice emerges. But by the time they reach this stage, while singers are certainly aware of the sounds they are making, they are almost an afterthought, secondary to an appreciation of the sensations they are feeling.

This transition from hearing to feeling is the natural result of returning from the technical monitoring of the voice to intuitively sensing and experiencing it, but *consciously* attending to this shift is also incredibly important. To begin, it allows you to ascertain whether or not what you are hearing is actually a sound, and what you are feeling is actually a sensation.

This might seem obvious on an intellectual level; after all, they are two very different senses: the ear hears and the body feels. But in singing, these two experiences get confused all the time. Clients often complain about "funny feelings" when their voices are actually making odd sounds or are going off pitch, or, more commonly, will claim to hear sounds that they do not like when, in fact, it is unfamiliar feelings (usually a sense of freedom or being out of control) that they do not care for.[13] Problems arise when a singer tries to address this uncared for feeling or sound, when in fact it is the other that is causing or indicative of the problem.

Placement and Resonance

In addition to making sure we understand the distinction between feeling and sound, we must take care that what we are hearing is an actual representation of the sound we are creating. While this is true for every singer, it is particularly so in classical and "legit" singing, where placement and resonance are being utilized.[14] What a singer hears inside the head is often very different from what the voice actually sounds like in the room. Covering and tightening can sound like a big and warm tone inside a singer's head, while a thin, faraway sound in the singer's ears is often resonating and filling the room with color and warmth. To further complicate matters, this sound issue often gets confused with physical sensation, and I have had these aural experiences described to me as, "It feels like a warm and rich tone in my head" or "It feels faraway and thin."

Even without resonance and placement, the ears can incorrectly convince singers that bad sounds are good simply for their familiarity, and that good ones are not good singing because they sound different and new. The ears, like the body, recognize and categorize the sounds and engagements a singer makes. And, like the body, the ears want to return not necessarily to what sounds better, but what they best remember and have linked with their definition of singing.

These challenges begin to be resolved when a singer makes a conscious effort to focus primarily on the physical sensations of vocal production rather than on the sound. This does not mean that you should not pay attention to the sound of your voice when you sing, but your perspective will necessarily change. You will be more like an insightful, but distant, observer rather than a critic sitting on the collar of your shirt. Going back to an earlier metaphor, eventually the gentle sensation of the touch will replace and become as strong as the stinging smack. In time, you will hear your voice fully and clearly, while maintaining the safe distance necessary to achieve and keep it so.

Another trick of the ears often leads people to believe that a more beautiful voice or seemingly complicated performance is correspondingly difficult to achieve in the body. This is no truer than any of the other myths we have debunked so far. Remember this as we begin discussing stylization, and keep your focus on feeling rather than on sound.

Strengthening the Voice

Strengthening the voice does not necessarily require you to sing loud or hard. In fact, some of the best strengthening techniques are rather quiet and delicate; as discussed in the diaphragm section, it often requires more physical and mental energy to engage and sustain a quiet tone than a loud one. The strength I am referring to is in the *consistency of engagement*. A voice with a strong support mechanism that has been correctly and repeatedly engaged records that success in the mind and body, and is then able to engage at any time, with any range of emotion and at any volume.

Continuing to build upon earlier exercises, let's look at a slightly different approach to our ABC's:

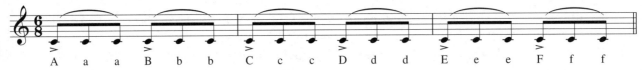

Punch each letter the first time around, then reduce the volume as you sing the second two, *while maintaining the same amount of support and energy*. If your throat is indeed relaxed and the exercise feels comfortable and open, play with both expanding the contrast between the loud and soft approaches to each letter (while maintaining a consistent support), and with seeing how far you can go on a single breath. Focus on how you experience the diaphragmatic and subglottal pressures in your body.

The Soft Palate

You more advanced singers may have noticed the movement of the soft palate that, hopefully, you were too distracted to consider engaging. For those unfamiliar with the soft palate, it is the soft, back part of the roof of your mouth, to which the visible M-shaped flap of skin, the uvula, is attached. To watch and feel it lift, look at the back of your throat the next time you yawn.

Singers raise and relax the soft palate for a variety of effects: to alter timbre, access resonation, create more space in the mouth, and affect certain guttural sounds. The deliberate lifting of the palate is a great tool in certain situations, though I contend—as with most of the vocal apparatus— that, given a relaxed and correctly engaged vocal system, the soft palate will move on its own as needed for optimal phonation in the majority of situations. In the next exercises, notice if and when the soft palate moves, as well as any effect on sensation or sound (and, for advanced singers, placement and resonance).

Let's expand upon the last exercise by taking a quick catch breath after every two or four letters, with the goal being to maintain the same feeling throughout the line. You are strengthening the body's ability to take in air while maintaining the integrity of the phrase, as well as strengthening the mind's resolve that breathing is a process requiring no extraneous or obstructive energy. While you will be focusing on when to breathe, do your best to avoid preparing or affecting the breath in any way:

Expand further upon this exercise by moving between the notes of the octave:

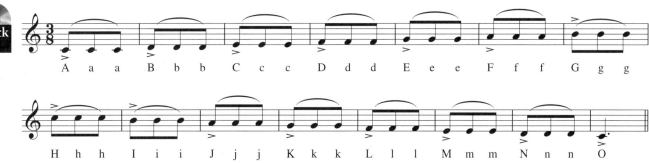

There are a few things to consider upon completing this exercise. First, did you feel a sense of apprehension at the idea of walking up the scale? Did it seem easier when you went back down? If this is the case, focus more on the speech of the letters and the pronunciation of each. You likely will notice that the exercise gets easier as your mind releases the technical idea of the specific pitches and their relationships to one another.

Diction

Something else to consider is whether certain consonants were easier to sing than the vowels. For many people this is the case, as the production of letters like B, C, and D begin with a burst of air that helps to fully engage the energy and sound, whereas the channel needs to be open and fully functional when the sound begins for A, E, and I. Our earlier examples of non-voiced consonants, as well as the "sh," "s," and lip trill exercises, help to make a habit of properly engaging and maintaining strong support and an open channel of air. Muscle memory can then transfer this association of engagement when the tools and consonants are taken away, resulting in a consistently strong and connected support. The use,

Register Shifts

You may have noticed at one point during the last exercise that your voice "broke," or shifted into a different sound or place. On Track 45 of the CD, you can hear this in my voice in the ascending line on the letter G and the descending on the letter I. This is called a register shift, one from the chest voice to the head voice in this case, and is a point at which the vocal folds essentially need to shift into a different position to continue their progression to higher notes. As we discussed in chapter three, the location of the shift not only varies from voice to voice, but from context to context. My voice shifted on a G above middle C in this exercise, even though my shift in performance tends to be somewhere around a B or C in the same register.

The Head and Chest Voices

This shift is one of the most crucial areas of the voice for singers in nearly every genre of music. In addition to being physically necessary to access a larger number of notes, singers also use and even consciously exaggerate it to express and evoke emotion. Justin Timberlake uses the audible shifting back and forth between the head and chest registers frequently for this purpose, as does LeAnn Rimes in the chorus of "Blue."[15] Maxwell exclusively uses his head (or falsetto) voice in Kate Bush's "This Woman's Work" with great emotional effect before returning briefly to his chest voice at the end of the song.[16] Whitney Houston makes the artistic choice to use first her head voice, then chest voice, on the choruses of "I Will Always Love You."[17]

The use of the shift to convey and evoke emotion is also a popular practice on Broadway today. The character of Maureen in *Rent* shifts noticeably between her head and chest voices in the chorus of "Out Tonight,"[18] as does Moritz's character in *Spring Awakening* at the end of the phrase, "I don't do sadness,"[19] though the shift in the Broadway world is generally much more inaudible. Called "the blend," the head voice is placed and strengthened to sound like a chest tone and the chest tone placed and lightened to sound like the head voice, resulting in a seamless sound that covers the entire range without a perceptible break.

While the shift can be a great tool of expression for Broadway and commercial singers, it is often a real challenge in terms of both ideal production and vocal health. Unlike classical and "legit" singers, who develop and use the head tone throughout their range, even in low registers, many commercial and theater singers primarily develop the chest voice at the expense of the head tone, creating not only an audible break, but two entirely distinct voices. The singer often then avoids the weak head voice and awkward shift, thereby encouraging the distinction. Commercial singers who want to correct this problem, along with Broadway singers who want to improve their "blend," will often try to smooth over the sound of their break by adversely affecting various muscles, rather than releasing the tension that contributed to the distinction and allowing the mechanism to strengthen properly. This causes further problems, and if continued, can strain and even damage the vocal folds.

You can choose to have a marked distinction between your head and chest voices, but in training, you still want the transition between the two to be as fluid and inaudible as possible. A great exercise for strengthening and streamlining vocal shift is the slide. I find that an "oo" or "ee" sound works best for many people, to which you can add a beginning consonant to help fully engage and open the support channel:

Some of you will hear a marked difference between the registers (demonstrated on Track 47), which this exercise will help to resolve. This is a rare time that I will encourage you to monitor sound rather than sensation, as the sound is more audible than the sensation noticeable, particularly in the voice box where the transition is actually occurring. Of course, it remains important not to affect musculature in an effort to vary the sound, only that you should be aware of it.[20]

If you have a discernible shift, without engaging any musculature, see if you can further relax your body and play around with the intensity of your air to blend the two "voices" more. Put away the idea of an exercise and instead imagine the sound of a fire engine; focus on maintaining a wide-open throat and a consistently engaged support mechanism. As just discussed, an audible shift is most often the result of either a lack of use or misuse, which will begin to be corrected by retraining the muscles, mind, and throat in their engagements. If you are a real belter and find yourself straining before shifting to a weak or airy head voice, I would recommend setting aside this kind of material for a while until the shift becomes more streamlined. Once the muscles responsible for the shift are retrained, you can return to your repertoire and create the desired sounds with a healthier approach.

Classical singers, including "legit" theater singers, often have the opposite problem. The head voice is usually very strong, and often can be brought down quite low in the speaking range. But the combination of an artificially lifted soft palate and a mental block against the chest register often keeps classical singers from a flexible musculature that allows the addition of a chest tone to their vocal arsenal.

To address this challenge, slide down the octave, making sure to transition to the chest voice at some point. This may require you to start the exercise substantially lower in your range:

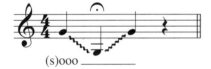

(s)ooo _____

I find that forward, open sounds like "say" can also be good choices for this exercise, as they keep the tone bright while limiting the possibility of it "falling back" and darkening, as on an incorrect "ah" or "oh":

seh _____

Linger on the lower notes, and observe whether it is a challenge for you to allow the palate to move at will. If so, try consciously to relax it down on the lowest note, and observe if, when, and how it lifts back up in the ascending line, taking note of placement and resonance as they occur naturally.

The Passaggio

In addition to the challenge of accessing a lower chest range, the classical singer's need to utilize higher notes than a commercial singer necessitates an additional shift within the head voice itself. Called the passage, or in the common Italian, the *passaggio*, this transition usually lies somewhere in women between a B and F above middle C. This is a particularly tricky area of the voice not only for the physiology, but also because it often corresponds with more conversational parts of the repertoire. A singer determined to articulate can actually interfere with the efficient use of this area of the voice, and instead should focus first on the liberation and strengthening of this register shift, using vowel modification to communicate the text.

To work on the *passaggio*, I find the vocal slide to again be a great tool. Move through the range on a natural and forward (meaning without any conscious placement or covering) "ah" or "eh" sound.

As always, take note of where and how your voice and body naturally want to make modifications, then work toward changing the shape of your vowels to keep this area as consistently wide open and comfortable as possible. When you work on the text of your repertoire, make sure not to compromise these sensations.

Any of the vocal slides we have discussed can also be done on a lip trill.

Agility

Agility is one of the biggest challenges for singers because of how complicated arpeggios (for the classical singer) or riffs and runs (for the commercial singer) sound. While these feats are—like most aspects of advanced vocalization—functions of a strong support system, freedom of air, and disciplined muscle memory, agility also requires a major amount of mental discipline, as well as a determined focus on feeling rather than hearing

As slides do not usually induce fear or present problems given the lack of articulated pitches, let's begin our look at agility this way. Setting aside attention to the shift, the goal here is simply to experience the slide as a sensation:

(s)ooo _____

Now, vary one physical component, and no mental component:

(s)ooo _____

While there is an audible difference between the slide up and walk down, take care to see whether any physical distinction you notice is truly physiological—or actually psychological, causing a physical engagement.

A survey of your speaking voice in an animated conversation will find you employing an approach similar to this and other agile vocal lines. The main physical difference is that, in riffs and arpeggios, we do not always have the benefit of constant reengagement (as with a consonant) to regulate the breath. Instead, we need to be strong enough to maintain a fully engaged and connected support. Let's understand this by looking once again at our ABC's in both thirds and fifths:

A B C D E F G H I J K L M N O P Q R S T U V double-U X Y Z

Try to make each letter clearly and evenly articulated. If you find yourself sliding between notes or are having trouble with the speed, use an emphasis on diction to help. You may also return to a few of the earlier diaphragm exercises to make sure your support system is connected and ready. Next, repeat the exercise at the same speed, but spread out the letters:

A_ B_ C_ D_ E_ F_ G_ H_ I_____ J_____ K_____ L_____ M

Those with the desire to control have a very hard time with agility in both practice and performance. In an effort to hit each note, their intellectual determination often shifts the focus away from the air to the throat, which hinders the freedom necessary to succeed. But when the mind is ready and willing to observe, rather than to control a riff or arpeggio, agility emerges increasingly, which muscle memory can then make into a habit.

Imitation

I have found in recent years that agility has become more naturally common in singers, which I attribute to the transition in popularity from artists who could sing loud and long to those who could riff and run. Mariah Carey's entrance onto the music scene in the early '90s is what I remember as the beginning of this transition.

Not only did this change the vocal style of the contemporary music we listened to, but the way we sang as well. Children who grew up singing along with Mariah Carey, Christina Aguilera, and the like, are often more able to sound like them: as with accents, the powers of the ear and imitation are strong. Those who were exposed to and learned to embody these stylizations as habits still have them as tools today.

While the potential ramifications of this concept are certainly intriguing—Can hearing and singing along with opera exclusively as a young child help begin to affect vocal musculature and resonance to that end? How many languages can be learned if a child is exposed early enough?—so are some of the practical limitations. I am always fascinated by clients who can sing incredible riffs while being entirely unable to perform a variety of agility exercises similar to those we looked at moments ago.

What this tells me is that agility born of observation and imitation does not always indicate a full ability to be vocally agile. Like people who can flawlessly play only one or two songs on the guitar or piano that they studied as a child, some singers intuitively and physically captured isolated experiences in childhood that stayed with them into adulthood. These singers are no more able to transfer this isolated "knowledge" of agility to current vocal production than the adult piano or guitar player is able to masterfully perform a different song. Only those who sang with agility often and in a variety of contexts seem to embody the tool today and have a mechanism able to support agility across the board. Whether in childhood or in adulthood, the goal remains the same: to foster an intuitive physical and mental understanding of agility so that the vocal freedom developed is not an isolated one.

Emotion

Emotion, like agility, is a function of air, rather than a direct manipulation of musculature. Still, many people engage a host of unnecessary vocal tensions when interpreting a song, exacerbated by an inability to differentiate between an emotional *sound* and an emotional *performance*.

Like hearing and feeling, these two things get confused all the time. In an effort to give an emotional-looking performance, singers often engage

Emotion, like agility, is a function of air, rather than a direct manipulation of musculature.

physical expressions that in time become habits unto themselves, encouraging tension and interfering with their natural method of sound production. The head tilt conveying whimsy, the passionate arch of the neck, and the exaggerated brow movements that were once intentional choices are now physical and vocal habits that the singer cannot kick.

You may have the most expressive face in the world, but can you create the same amount of vocal emotion deadpan in the mirror? Like physical expression, all vocal choices must be choices as well. There are singers who can belt out a song loud and free, but can they bring it down to an intimate whisper, or sing it in a convincing head tone? The distinct challenges of physical expression and emotional sound must be separated and developed independently. Once this has happened, they can then be brought back together to vastly improve your physical and vocal range of performance possibilities.

Interpretation as a Vocal Tool

In terms of the vocal aspect, I find that the best emotional work is done within the context of a song. Not only are scales and exercises just not as exciting, the more relevant and integrated your training can be, the better prepared you are for performance. Looking again at "Amazing Grace" as an example, begin by speaking the words straight and on a single tone:

When we take melody and rhythm away, two things happen. First, any corresponding physical tension that we might have been carrying often dissipates when we stop "singing." Second, we often realize that we have been relying on both melody and rhythm to create an emotional context, rather than consider what we as vocalists and communicators can bring to the table.

Once we break this habit, it becomes obvious in most songs almost instantly that both the melody and rhythm create space for the words and singer to really say something. Let's first consider the rhythmic variable:

Taking care that any added emotion is exclusively vocal, now allow your mind and voice to return to the melody, itself another revelation that serves to expand the meaning and our ability to express it:

I find fascinating the precarious placement of "grace" on the third degree of the scale, and the word "sound" resonating in the lowest part of the musical line rather than as a high exclamation. To me, the song is a pendulum of melody and meaning that begins its swing in a wide arc, only to bring the extremes of pitch and the human condition (being lost and being found) together on the tonic at the end of the verse: "was blind, but now I see." Meaning is waiting in every song to be used for a fuller and richer communication. Challenge yourself to seek and incorporate it always, not just on the eve of an audition or performance.

Emotion in Physical Performance

This approach is also crucial in physical performance. The common problem singers have with not knowing what do to with their hands and arms is one of many caused by the whole person not being fully engaged in the meaning of a piece. Therefore, always approach a song as a performance—even in rehearsal, even in a

The greatest performers make us feel comfortable, no matter what emotion they are experiencing or expressing.

voice lesson. When the time comes to actually perform, you will be well-rehearsed at embodying the character both physically and mentally.

When a character has not been fully explored or integrated, it is impossible to be truly authentic or believable in a performance or audition. Many of us are not fully comfortable in our own physical and mental bodies, making it an additional challenge to become so in someone else's. I have watched clients excel and convince me completely in comedic and character roles, only to turn uncomfortable and awkward in a sexier or more vulnerable piece.

The greatest performers make us feel comfortable, no matter what emotion they are experiencing or expressing. It is their personal, physical, and emotional vulnerability that makes us connect, and the lack of it that holds so many performers back. When the actor onstage is wrestling with authenticity, we too wrestle with our ability to believe him.

Fine Tuning

Trouble Spots

Even the most talented, natural, and intuitive singers occasionally have issues that require a bit of attention. Often the cause is obvious, and other times a glitch will come out of nowhere, with no apparent explanation. Problem solving is obviously a very individual matter, but in a song, changing the context is generally a good way to begin breaking bad habits, as well as to prevent new ones from forming.

Starting with thirds or fifths (moving on to octaves and jazz and other voicings as you get more advanced), sing through the lyric and see whether it helps to shift any negative physical associations you may have. Also, look for any mental tension you may experience on the approach to areas that do or might give you trouble in the musical context:

An added benefit of resolving trouble spots in this way is the further reinforcement of the positive habits we have been nurturing. While our minds are focused on problematic melodic aspects of a specific song, our bodies are simultaneously strengthening the diaphragm, as well as conditioning the shift and agility.

Changing the key of a song can also help to redefine negative associations. Moving a song up or down a whole- or half-step, while demonstrating that a particular note is not inherently problematic, might not help you release the tension you have built up around the note. In such cases, I often have clients sing the song a major third or perfect fourth up or down from the key they would usually sing it in.

In the lower key, the fear of the "high" note and impulse to tighten up on it will still be there, though it will no longer seem physically or intellectually necessary (not that it ever was). Repeating this approach in the lower range a number of times will help reinforce this new confident association, which can then be transferred back to the original key. A singer then realizes that it is an increase in air and strength along with a shift of approach that is required, rather than apprehension of a certain note or passage.

In the higher key, singers are generally so preoccupied with the troublesome "high" note or notes that they fail to see that more, and perhaps most, of the notes of the song are now in that same feared range. In addition, this drastic alteration of key will usually help demonstrate (as does the shift to the lower one), that it is perhaps a "fear of heights" in general, exacerbated by an insufficient and/or incorrect approach in support, that is the fundamental problem, rather than a specific pitch.

Melodic Context

Often, problems we encounter are not functions of the voice, but of the structure of the song itself. There are two issues in particular I have seen plague even the best of singers, both demonstrated by the following example:

While this line does not look particularly difficult, Renée had trouble every time she reached this first part of the chorus. Interestingly, it was not the higher notes that caused her problems, but the initial lower one, which tended to sound tight and slightly under pitch. She also had trouble with the chorus's final word, "all," which, given her consistent ability to achieve free and beautifully sustained notes, was unusual:

Regarding the first problem, the voice and mind generally focus most on getting to the perceived highlight of a line. In this case, "say you care" is the focus melodically and rhythmically, leaving "don't" neglected mentally—and, therefore, physically. We have spent a good deal of time talking about the importance of maintaining support throughout a phrase, regardless of how quiet or insignificant a part of that phrase may seem, and this is a great example of that point. The verse ends, and the mind and body prepare to shift to the chorus, leaving its seemingly inconsequential first note lost in the shuffle.

In order to break this habit, we altered the context that had created it. By rearranging the first two notes as shown below, the first word became a highlight of the line, thus altering the "inconsequential" association:

For Renée, this new configuration changed not only the melodic perspective of the song, but the emotional one, which she personally and physically embraced. By having Renée then repeat the first two pitches in this configuration, her muscle memory was simultaneously practicing the correct relationship from low to high on the second and third pitches, while she remained focused exclusively on the new relationship of the first two:

Going back to the original melody of song was easy, as both her body and mind had altered their associations and created ones that were more positive.

Vowel Modification

We previously touched upon the cause of Renée's second concern in the non-voiced to voiced consonant section, as well in the discussions of the classical slide and *passaggio*. Certain words and letters cause problems for singers, due to the amount or type of space they require in the mouth, as well as tongue placement. Back-sounding vowels like "o" (boat), "ah" (father), and "uh" (some) are common culprits, as are letters like L, N, M, and R, which require both the diminishing of oral cavity space as well as a partial impediment to the flow of air. This was a secondary problem on the word "don't," as well as the main culprit on the final word of the chorus, "all."

We were able to correct both problems using vowel modification, a very important tool for singers in fine-tuning their performance. This is particularly true for classical and "legit" singers, who need to carefully balance the integrity of pronunciation and the maintenance of an optimal amount of space in the mouth.

For "don't," we started by changing the shape dramatically, singing instead "day say you care." This helped Renée's muscle memory and conscious mind to realize that the problem was less the note and more the word on it, exacerbated until recently by a lack of sufficient energy. Once we had altered both the physical and mental associations, we moved through a range of other vowels, returning eventually to "don't" while maintaining the openness of "day."

While not problematic for Renée, the same approach could also work in the treatment of both "care" and the more closed "you" that precedes it. Singing through the line on the words "they say I know" will show you the ease with which the line is able to be sung. Vowels can then be modified to maintain this sense of openness on the true lyric.

Vowel modification often involves the "faking" of words and letters as well. For example, while you could not say, "Doe say you care" without people thinking you were talking about a deer or suffering from a head cold, removing the "n" and "t" from a sung line barely registers as a change. We applied this principle to the last note in the chorus, replacing "all" with "ah." At first, Renée still encountered problems because her body remembered the closing down on the L, even when it was no longer there. We needed to completely change the context a few times, singing an entirely different word at the end of the line that encouraged openness (say, pay, fly, tie), so that when we returned to the "ah," her body was able to make a new association and record it as habit. With a healthy and wide-open "ah" sound, a simple flick of her tongue at the very end of the phrase would convince anyone that she was singing the word "all."

Silent Learning

A final tool that works beautifully for both beginning and professional singers is what I call Diaphragmatic Learning. As we touched upon in the Emotion section, it is important to fully physically engage at all times in every song in order to form proper muscular habits and associations. This doesn't mean that you must sing every song loudly, but rather, that you must be physically committed to every performance.

Many singers are disciplined with this tool in both practice and performance, but not in learning a new piece. When singers hear or sight read through a song for the first time, often they will "fake sing" their way through it, pulling off of their support and pinching their throats to "find" and "touch" the notes just to "get a feel" for it.

The problem with this method of learning is that muscle memory is unable to tell the difference between "learning" and "singing" a song. Two or three times of half-singing through a piece, and the muscles are already well on their way to forming unhealthy associations and engagements both because the support isn't properly engaged, and the technical mind is front and center in the process of acquiring this type of new information. This is particularly true with sight reading, where the up-and-down visual associations tend to encourage the same up-and-down motion with the neck.

My solution is to have a singer listen to a piece of music before sight reading or "fake-singing" through it. By listen, I mean not only once or twice, but fully learning the piece in complete silence and stillness. Once this is done, I go a step further and ask that they listen to the piece no longer with their ears, but with their diaphragms. This might seem like a strange request, but when singers focus exclusively on how the song will feel in their support system, they are no longer thinking of what it might feel like in their throats. After they have mastered the sound-as-feeling of the song, and finally open their mouths to sing, the proper associations are in place and the results are marvelous.

Conclusion

As we have discussed throughout the book, the process of vocal development is an individual one. Like learning and life, we see and hear the wisdom and whispers of the world around us when we are ready, when the messages present themselves in a way that we can and want to understand. If you feel confused or unclear about anything we have discussed, particularly in the areas where we nurtured the intuitive mind by tricking the technical mind, go back and see if another reading or run through the CD will provide more insight now that your mind and body have had a chance to consider and experience singing this way. Revisiting the exercises, in addition to developing and strengthening muscle memory, will, over time, offer additional and more advanced insights as you increase your intuitive awareness and ability to focus on specific aspects of the vocal mechanism and production.

It is my sincere hope that what we have discussed here will be beneficial to you on your own vocal and personal journey. If you have further questions or any thoughts you would like to share, please feel free to contact me through one of the websites listed on page 95. It would be my pleasure to do whatever I can to help you discover your best voice.

Endnotes

Chapter 1

1. The John F. Kennedy Center for the Performing Arts, Washington, D.C., April 19, 1998.

2. Tim Page, "Andrea Bocelli: Wan of a Kind. The Tenor's Special Effect Proves Limited," *Washington Post*, April 21, 1998, Style section.

3. John Newton, "Amazing Grace" (1779), public domain.

4. The notion that the classical voice is the only correct and healthy style in which to sing is a widely held philosophy of most university music programs. There are a number of musical theater and jazz programs in North America, but I have found that even the top ones have yet to share the same level of recognition and reputation as classical music schools and conservatories around the world.

5. Sadly, overtones of condescension toward other types of music often accompany the classical-only approach. I myself succumbed to this mentality in my freshman and sophomore years, criticizing pop and R&B singers that only a year or two earlier I had learned from and admired.

6. T.S. Eliot, "Little Gidding," *Four Quartets* (Chicago: Harcourt Brace & Co., 1943).

Chapter 2

1. John F. Kennedy, commencement address, Yale University, New Haven, CT, June 11, 1962.

2. This does not include screaming, as in certain types of heavy metal, hardcore punk, post-hardcore, and emo. If approached correctly, however, screaming often can be done with no harm to the vocal instrument.

3. Mildred J. Hill and Patty S. Hill, "Happy Birthday to You," Copyright © 1935 (Renewed) Summy-Birchard Music, a Division of Summy-Birchard, Inc.

4. The arytenoid cartilages, with the help of the corresponding musculature, spread and bring together the back of the vocal folds to create voiced and unvoiced (whispered) sound.

5. Between the ages of two and three, based on environment, areas of the brain begin to develop that can inhibit a child's natural pleasure seeking and creativity.

6. All client names have been changed.

Chapter 3

1. David Joseph Bohm (1917–1992), American-born quantum physicist speaking to Joseph Jaworski in *Synchronicity: The Inner Path of Leadership* (San Francisco: Berrett-Koehler Publishers, 1996), p. 174.

2. I believe that a large part of human beings' deep emotional connections with their pets comes from the inability to rely on our primary interactive communication tool—language—therefore requiring the development of a multitude of very powerful recessive and intuitive communication abilities.

3. Proprioception is a sense internal to the body that tells the mind where various parts of the body are located in relation to each other. Even with your eyes closed, you can tell if your arm is above your head or at your side, or if your leg is bent or straight. It also helps us sense when or whether the body is moving and at what rate.

4. Anthony Robbins, *Notes from a Friend: A Quick and Simple Guide to Taking Control of Your Life* (New York: Fireside Books, 1995), p. 70.

5. Developed by John Grinder and Richard Bandler at the University of California, Santa Cruz in the 1970s.

6. Susan Jeffers, *Feel the Fear and Do It Anyway* (New York: Ballantine Books, 1988).

7. If you have difficulty with loss of voice, reduction of range, or extended hoarseness and discomfort, consult an otolaryngologist to establish whether you have a physical problem that may require rest and/or medical attention.

8. The simple act of singing a song after telling yourself that the high notes are low and vice versa will astound you; even that singular thought—that singular shift in NLP—after a lifetime of reaching will alter the way your body treats the notes.

9. See chapter seven for further discussion and examples of vocal sliding.

Chapter 4

1. Chuang Tse was one of the original Taoist writers. Translated in Benjamin Hoff's *The Te of Piglet* (New York: Penguin Books, 1993), p. 133.

2. Of course, more parental attention and losing the common diet rich in sugar, caffeine, and processed foods would have helped as well, as they would any child.

3. Doris Lessing, *The Four-Gated City* (New York: Harper Perennial, 1995; originally published in 1969), p. 111.

4. In the next chapter, we will discuss the brain and its relevance to how you learn and process information.

5. The *Harry Potter* series is comprised of seven novels by J.K. Rowling, published by Scholastic Press (United States), 1997–2007.

6. Henry David Thoreau, *Life without Principle* (1863). Quoted by Benjamin Hoff in *The Te of Piglet* (New York: Penguin Books, 1993), p. 65.

7. John Paul Schaefer, *The Ansel Adams Guide: Basic Techniques of Photography* (Boston: Little, Brown and Company, 1992).

8. Stephen R. Covey, *The 7 Habits of Highly Effective People: Powerful Lessons in Personal Change* (New York: Free Press, 1989, 2004) p. 235ff.

Chapter 5

1. Except for approximately 5% of the population, for which the right hemisphere is dominant. From Daniel J. Levitin's *This Is Your Brain on Music* (New York: Plume, 2007), p. 124.

2. Even the simplest of daily activities, such as the perception of sound, requires a coordination of at least ten dominant and non-dominant areas of the brain, making the more complex functions of singing and learning dizzying in complexity. Dr. James H. Fallon (Professor of Psychiatry, Human Behavior, and Neuroscience at the University of California, Irvine), in conversation with the author, January 2008.

3. I am generalizing to illustrate common differences between the technical and creative minds, not in an attempt to categorize and define everyone. Some people are highly technical in their way of thinking, save for certain and specific areas of activity when they shift to a more creative mode.

4. Brain scans show that the *corpus callosum*, which connects the right and left hemispheres, is often larger in professional musicians than in the rest of the population, suggesting greater interconnectivity. See *The Cognitive Neuroscience of Music* by Isabelle Peretz and Robert J. Zatorre (Oxford: Oxford University Press, 2003).

5. Via the mirror neuron system. From the author's conversations with Dr. James H. Fallon.

6. The dorsal and orbital prefrontal cortices, respectively. From the author's conversations with Dr. James H. Fallon.

7. Erik Erikson and others have speculated that society's outcome-oriented, technical approach forces children to speak and read too soon, before their minds have the chance to "behold" intuitively the world around them. This inhibits optimal experiencing and cognitive understanding.

8. Joseph Jaworski, *Synchronicity: The Inner Path of Leadership* (San Francisco: Berrett-Koehler Publishers, 1996), p. 45.

9. Ibid., p. 54.

10. William F. Russell, *Second Wind: The Memoirs of an Opinionated Man* (New York: Simon & Schuster, 1991).

11. Bryan Reeves, *Life, Electromagnetic Energy and Your Well-Being* (Miami: The Teslar Corporation, 2005).

12. Valerie V. Hunt, *Infinite Mind: Science of the Human Vibrations of Consciousness* (Malibu: Malibu Publishing, 2000).

13. Betty Edwards, *Drawing on the Right Side of the Brain* (New York: Tarcher/Putnam, 1979).

14. In dementia cases, people with injuries to the inhibitors (dorsal and orbital prefrontal cortices) who have previously never touched a paintbrush or instrument suddenly become adept at art and music. B. L. Miller, J. Cummings, F. Mishkin, K. Boone, F. Prince, M. Ponton, and C. Cotman, "Emergence of Artistic Talent in Frontotemporal Dementia," *Neurology 51* (1998), pp. 978–982.

15. While the ability to process information in a sensory and creative manner is innate in all of us and imperative for optimal singing, inherent talent is another matter. Scientists still debate and research its origins.

16. The recently discovered mirror neuron system is responsible for the "witnessing" that we experience, beginning in childhood. It processes and internalizes activity, both personally experienced and externally observed, by an individual, but only in 3-D and in real time. This helps to explain why hands-on teaching methods are generally more effective than 2-D teaching tapes and videos. From the author's conversations with Dr. Fallon.

17. Jaworski, p. 82.

18. The same is true of headphones in studio recording.

Chapter 6

1. James Redfield, *The Tenth Insight: Holding the Vision* (New York: Warner Books, 1996), p. 57.

2. Franklin D. Roosevelt, first inaugural address, Washington, D.C., March 4, 1933.

3. Susan Jeffers' book *Feel the Fear and Do it Anyway* is a fantastic resource on the subject of fear. Her thesis is that fear has three stages, the deepest—and most important one—being "I can't handle it." Once we understand that everything in life is manageable, fear dissipates.

4. Joseph Campbell (1904–1987), noted author and professor of mythology and religion at Sarah Lawrence College.

5. Chuang Tse. Translated in Benjamin Hoff's *The Te of Piglet* (New York: Penguin Books, 1993), p. 110.

6. William Shakespeare, *As You Like It*, Act 2, scene 7.

7. The necessary use of headphones in studio recording can be an added distraction.

8. With the sound no longer resonating in the air, the mind often has to actively accommodate for variances that are unconsciously dealt with in a natural setting.

9. The boosting or cutting of certain frequencies to achieve a desired tonality.

10. The use of an electronic device to reduce the dynamic range of a signal (balance loud and soft) by inversely raising and lowering its volume level.

11. Robert Wright, in correspondence with the author, January 2008.

12. Frequency masking is the inability to hear certain instruments or voices because they are covered up by those occupying the same frequencies.

13. Panning is the adjusting of the instruments and voices to the left or right of center within a stereo mix.

Chapter 7

1. Lao Tsu, *Tao Te Ching*.

2. *Merriam-Webster's Collegiate Dictionary, Eleventh Edition* (Springfield: Merriam-Webster, Inc., 2005).

3. Richard Bach, *Jonathan Livingston Seagull* (New York: Avon Books, 1970), p. 104.

4. It is preferable to drink room-temperature water, because cold water shocks the system, adversely affecting the tissues, membranes, and muscles of the throat.

5. While water is imperative to the vocal mechanism and body in terms of hydration, the water you swallow does not pass through the vocal folds. Singers often sip water in an effort to "clear their throats" when, in fact, every time you swallow, the epiglottis covers the entrance to the trachea (where the vocal folds are), redirecting all ingested substances to the stomach via the esophagus.

6. As discussed in chapter three, it is a reflexive muscle that engages automatically when we take in or expel air.

7. The lack of images of the vocal anatomy here, as well as of the brain in chapter five, is intentional. Before seeing any diagrams and pictures, it is imperative that you feel and experience your vocal mechanism—and the mind that runs it—as you did as a child. This prevents the tendency to focus on physiology and musculature, which can detract from the intuitive process.

8. While most speak exclusively of the diaphragm when it comes to breath support (as we will here for the sake of simplicity), in actuality, a system of muscles is engaged in conjunction with the diaphragm to enable breathing, speaking, and properly supported singing, particularly in exhalation.

9. There is no deliberate pause in the in-out cycle of the natural breath.

10. For many people, the experience of subglottal pressure is higher in the vocal tract, if it is noticed at all.

11. Other voiced consonants include L, M, N, and R. These will be discussed in a later section, as their phonation presents some specific challenges.

12. Most of the musical notation in this chapter is in the key of C major for the sake of visual simplicity, but feel free—as I have on the CD—to sing the exercises wherever your voice feels comfortable. Ideally, work through these vocalizations without a piano or key reference, as it will help to further distinguish this experience from a traditional training situation. Your technical mind will have less to cling to and, therefore, less tension to physically reinitiate based on potential mental and muscle memories of past experiences.

13. Peter, in chapter six, is a good example.

14. Resonance is the natural process by which a vocal sound is amplified. Classically trained singers, especially, develop this technique, using resonance to project and color their vocal timbre. Placement is the natural ability to direct the voice into certain areas of the body, face, or mask to achieve a desired resonance, projection, or tonal effect, which is cultivated toward a positive end.

15. Bill Mack, "Blue," Copyright © 1966 (Renewed) by Fort Knox Music Inc. and Trio Music Company.

16. Kate Bush, "This Woman's Work," Copyright © 1988 by Kate Bush Music Ltd. All rights controlled and administered by Screen Gems-EMI Music Inc.

17. Dolly Parton, "I Will Always Love You," Copyright © 1973 (Renewed 2001) by Velvet Apple Music.

18. Jonathan Larson, "Out Tonight," Copyright © 1996 by Finster & Lucy Music Ltd. Co. All rights controlled and administered by Universal Music Corp.

19. Duncan Sheik and Steven Sater, "I Don't Do Sadness," Copyright © 2006 by Universal Music-Careers, Duncan Sheik Songs, Happ Dog Music and Kukuzo Productions, Inc.

20. You will likely notice that the shift into the head voice is usually accompanied by the automatic lifting of the soft palate.

The Art of Singing
CD Track Listing

About the Author

Jennifer Hamady has not only performed, toured, and recorded with some of music's top names, but has coached many of them as well. Her thorough knowledge of the voice, coupled with a unique understanding of how best to communicate with singers and creators, has attracted a clientele of recording artists, Broadway performers, and television actors, many of them recipients of Grammy Awards, CMA Awards, and Emmy Awards. Focusing on the integrated individual as the instrument of communication, Jennifer is renowned for bringing out the vocal and personal best of those she works with.

Jennifer can be reached at:
www.jenniferhamady.com
www.theartofsinging.com

"Jennifer's book simply confirms her abilities in discerning the fundamentals of life. Powerfully insightful, her treatment of fear has immediate application and revolutionary impact, as she has identified the core problems that undermine the full performance of so many people. I have no doubt that her book will have enormous positive impact on a wide cross-section of people."

> — Dr. Amii-Omara Ottunu, Chair,
> UNESCO Institute of Human Rights,
> University of Connecticut

"The Mother Teresa of voice liberation."

> —Ben E., singer/songwriter, Colorado

"I have found my voice with Jennifer, a natural, healthy voice that was buried under years of bad habits, muscle tension, faulty technique, unhelpful definitions of singing, and negative experiences."

> —Vivian W., performance artist, New York, NY

"She's written the singer's version of *The Secret*. Oprah would be proud!"

> —Clair R., singer/songwriter, New York

"Jennifer has worked with me to begin my entrance into freedom—not just as a musician, artist, and singer—but as a person, spirit, and soul."

—Lia M., Berklee College of Music, Boston, MA

"The same loving, inquisitive spirit I experienced with Eloise Ristad shines through Jennifer Hamady's work."

—Ron Thompson, M.A.,
Masterful-Life Performance Psychologist, Vermont

"I can honestly say that I learned more from Jennifer in two weeks than from anyone else in my career as a singer and performer. I consider myself very fortunate to have had the opportunity to work with her."

—Chad Oliver, singer, Cirque du Soleil

"I'd never seen a force of joy, compassion, sharp-mindedness, grace, experience, and guts so captivating until I met Jennifer..."

—Jim F., singer/songwriter, Paris, France

"Working with Jennifer has been such a blessing... she opened up my voice in so many ways and taught me so many incredible techniques. I not only had fun working with her, but my voice is stronger and I am by far a much better singer and speaker. Thank you, Jennifer!"

—MacKenzie W., television actor, Los Angeles, CA

"Within the first coaching with Ms. Hamady, I developed a more comfortable approach to singing that sounded much closer to my natural voice that I unconsciously use every day in conversation. After a performance less than a week later, heard by strangers and friends alike, I received consistent observations attesting to my increased resonance and overall expression."

—Mike B., Julliard School of Music, New York, NY

"An incredible, beautiful and long-needed force to be reckoned with in the realm of vocal coaching and teaching."

—Kate F., Broadway performer, New York, NY

"Jennifer embodies every principle that she teaches, and her example is inspirational."

—Melissa G., recording artist, New York, NY

"A rare gem of a musician, teacher, and human being."

—John Briggs, Vice President, ASCAP

"A one-in-a-million find... we are talking about a brilliant and truly special person."

—Dr. James Fallon, Department of Psychiatry and
Human Behavior, Brain Imagining Center &
Professor Emeritus, Department of Anatomy and
Neurobiology, University of California, Irvine

"Fly, run, or swim to wherever this woman is... you will not regret it!"

—Rachel K., recording artist, Nashville, TN